Writing Short Stories

Are you struggling to write a short story?

Or keen to try, but unsure where to start?

You want to learn from published writers, but don't know how you can?

Writing Short Stories is the solution.

Ideal for those new to the genre or for anyone who wishes to improve their technique, this guide will help you to achieve your full potential as a short-story writer.

Each chapter of the book:

*   introduces key aspects of the craft of short-story writing, including structure, dialogue, characterization, viewpoint, narrative voice and more;
*   shows how a wide variety of published writers have approached the short-story genre, in order to deepen the insights you gain from your own work;
*   gets you writing, with a series of original, sometimes challenging and always rewarding, exercises that can be tackled alone or adapted for use in a group;
*   encourages you to be inventive, to break writing habits and to try something new, by showing the diversity of the short-story genre, from cyberpunk to social observation.

Ailsa Cox draws on her experience as a writer to provide essential information on drafting and editing as well as a rich Resources section, which lists print and online journals that accept the work of new writers. Whether you're writing as part of a course, in a workshop group or at home alone, this book will equip and inspire you to write better short stories.

Ailsa Cox is a published short-story writer and currently teaches Creative Writing at Edge Hill College in the United Kingdom.

Writing Short Stories

Ailsa Cox

Routledge
Taylor & Francis Group

LONDON AND NEW YORK

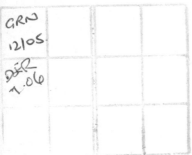

First published 2005
by Routledge
2 Park Square, Milton Park, Abingdon, Oxon, OX14 4RN

Simultaneously published in the USA and Canada
by Routledge
270 Madison Ave, New York, NY 10016

Routledge is an imprint of the Taylor & Francis Group

© 2005 Ailsa Cox

Typeset in Times by RefineCatch Limited, Bungay, Suffolk
Printed and bound in Great Britain by
TJ International Ltd, Padstow, Cornwall

British Library Cataloguing in Publication Data
A catalogue record for this book is available from the British Library

Library of Congress Cataloging in Publication Data
Cox, Ailsa.
Writing short stories/Ailsa Cox.
p.cm.
1. Short story—Authorship. I. Title.

PN3373.C67 2005
808.3′1—dc22

2005003646

ISBN 0–415–30386–9 (hbk)
ISBN 0–415–30387–7 (pbk)

Contents

Acknowledgements

My thanks first of all to Sue Roe and Livi Michael, who made this book possible. Thanks to the many fellow writers, colleagues and students who have shared ideas with me over the years, especially John Ashbrook, Elizabeth Baines, David Craig, Clare Hanson, Marian McCraith, Graham Mort, Anita Phillips and Marion Shaw. I am grateful to Gitte Mose, at the Danish Institute for Advanced Studies in the Humanities for information about hyperfiction, and to all at the Oslo Short Fiction Conference 2003. My editor at Routledge, Liz Thompson, and her assistants, Diane Parker and Kate Parker have been very patient and supportive. And finally, love and thanks to Tom Cox and Tim Power.

Introduction

Most fiction writers start with the short story. It gives them the opportunity to find their own voice, to learn the fundamentals of narrative composition, and, most importantly, to produce a complete piece of work over a limited timescale. If you're aiming for a professional career, you can make your breakthrough with publication in literary magazines, on radio or through the major competitions open to unpublished manuscripts, such as the Stand competition, the Flannery O'Connor award and the Raymond Carver award. Muriel Spark first got herself noticed by winning a competition in the London *Observer*. Thirty years later, William Gibson was commissioned to write a novel on the strength of a single story, 'Burning Chrome'.

Yet the short story is not just apprentice work. Many great prose writers, including Grace Paley, Katherine Mansfield and Raymond Carver, never published a novel. Even established novelists turn back to short fiction when they feel the need to refresh their talents. Peter Carey says writing short stories helps him take new risks. In a recent radio interview, he compared turning out a story to building a shed – a small, self-contained project you can take pride in. Kate Atkinson says that working on short stories restored her joy and playfulness in writing after producing three novels. But, as Atkinson stresses, 'the story is a genre in its own right, not the little sister of the novel' (Atkinson 2003b). A tightly concentrated form, it offers boundless scope for linguistic virtuosity and formal experimentation. This is why it has been at the forefront of literary innovation, from Edgar Allan Poe to James Joyce and Jorge Luis Borges, Angela Carter and A. M. Holmes; and that is why so many writers produce their best work at this length.

However, many new writers approach their first story as if they were starting a novel. They haven't grasped that short fiction is a specific form, with its own requirements. But what exactly are these distinctive qualities and requirements? The search for a definition begins in the mid-nineteenth century with Poe, who famously declared that 'all high excitements are necessarily transient' (Poe 1966: 520). According to Poe, the intensity of short, concentrated forms read in one sitting increases their emotional impact. Because short stories are self-contained, they also display a dramatic unity, building swiftly towards resolution. Poe allies the short story with poetry and painting, referring to a 'unity of effect and impression' created by the close integration of language, imagery and form.

Poe's analysis has never been bettered, his concept of unity and completion providing the basis for almost all short-story theory. The contemporary writer and critic Joyce Carol Oates looks at it this way: 'My personal definition of the form is that it represents a concentration of imagination, and not an expansion; it *is* no more than 10,000 words; and, no matter its mysteries or experimental properties, it achieves closure – meaning that, when it ends, the attentive reader understands why' (Oates 1998: 47).

Novels are usually discursive; they enlarge or embroider or, as Oates would say, 'expand' on their theme. A short story distils or condenses. It captures the essence of an experience. Oates touches on another characteristic often singled out by commentators – an inclination towards the mysterious, the elusive or 'elliptical' (see Chapter 6 on 'ellipsis'). Raymond Carver refers to 'the things that are left out, that are implied, the landscape just under the smooth (but sometimes broken and unsettled) surface of things' (Carver 1994: 26). Elizabeth Bowen, Nadine Gordimer and William Boyd reaffirm an affinity with poetry. In a short story, every word counts – and more than that, belongs – precisely in its place. Short stories are arranged, not as visibly as lines of poetry, but according to their own internal architecture.

Yet even as I write these definitions, they slip away from me. What on earth do I mean, 'conceived spatially', 'internal architecture'? (I changed 'architecture to 'rhythms', then changed it back again; I wanted to imply something spatial on the page.) I had more to say about the short story and lyric poetry, about ambiguity, illumination and imagery, until I realized I was becoming hopelessly abstract. We can only talk about tendencies, in the most general terms. With every definition, exceptions spring to mind. Take Joyce Carol Oates's insistence on 10,000 words. What about Thomas Mann's 'Death in Venice' (28,770 words) or Joseph Conrad's 'Heart of Darkness' (37,746)? We might introduce another category, the 'novella', but whatever you call Alice Munro's 'The Love of a Good Woman', it still feels like a short story to me, intrinsically no different to anything else she has written. At the other end of the scale, is there a minimum length? Kafka's 'A Little Fable' weighs in at a mere eighty-seven words.

The problem with definitions is that they narrow down the options. The short story is a protean form, encompassing infinite variations and, just like the novel, shading into other genres. As writers, we need to recognize a special quality in short fiction without imposing rigid distinctions. It is often pointed out that short stories differ from novels because they are restricted to a limited time frame and to just one or two characters. As a general observation, this can be helpful to new writers, but there are numerous examples – Borges, for example – who contradict the rule.

The reason why short-story writers have been so preoccupied with generic classification is the question of status. Historically, the novel has been the dominant form, and it is still difficult to establish a literary career based purely on short fiction. A brief historical overview will tell us more about the short story's emergence as a genre, which has been largely shaped by its readership. In his time, Poe was pitting the short story against the wordy three-volume novels – many of them pirated from England – which filled the periodicals of his day. His plans to raise the profile of short fiction were part of a wider project to shake off the legacy of the Old World, replacing it with a dynamic magazine-based culture.

This link between modernity, the short story and the magazine continued into the late nineteenth and early twentieth century. Stories by European writers such as Maupassant, Flaubert, Turgenev and Chekhov were associated with advanced thought and literary endeavour. French Symbolism, which was largely inspired by Poe's aesthetic theories, helped to shape short fiction from Oscar Wilde to Katherine Mansfield. Thanks to technological advances and widespread literacy, magazines flourished on both sides of the Atlantic. In the days before radio or television, general-interest magazines were a major source of family entertainment. The thirty years between 1890 and 1920 were a golden age for the short story. World-famous authors such as Arthur Conan Doyle or Rudyard Kipling were paid enormous sums to increase magazines' circulation with a thrilling new adventure. The short story thrives when it is published, and many of the classic examples I have used date from this period.

Magazine exposure was also important to those less interested in popular success. As I explain in Chapter 2, early twentieth-century writers such as Mansfield, Joyce and Woolf rejected traditional plot-driven narrative, using their stories to capture fleeting impressions and changing states of consciousness. Joyce's concept of the 'epiphany' – a sudden flash of inner transformation – found its best expression in the short story, and hence the form became central to the modernist experiment. The writing was circulated through 'little' magazines – the *Dial*, the *Little Review*, the *English Review, Rhythm* – founded to promote the avant-garde. Run on a shoestring, usually short-lived, these were the forerunners of today's literary magazines, read mostly by a limited pool of subscribers. The large circulation magazines, publishing short stories alongside feature articles, have almost vanished.

Poe and many subsequent critics regarded the short story as quintessentially American. It is, in fact, a strongly international genre. I've already mentioned the role played by Maupassant and Chekhov. Even in the heyday of the American magazine, the most highly paid writer was an Englishman, Kipling, while Henry James, an American master, spent most of his life abroad in Europe. Expatriates and nomads have contributed greatly to the short story – the Canadian Mavis Gallant, writing from Paris, or Trinidadian-born V. S. Naipaul. Younger writers, such as Jhumpa Lahiri and Nell Freudenberger, cut across national borders, shifting between Bengal and Boston, New York and Bangkok.

But it is true to say that the short story has been more strongly nurtured in the USA than in most other countries. As Andrew Levy points out in *The Culture and Commerce of the American Short Story*, university writing programmes patronize the heirs of Edith Wharton, Ernest Hemingway, Eudora Welty and F. Scott Fitzgerald, running numerous magazines, web sites and small presses. These provide outlets for work from students, professors and 'emergent' writers, and where there are opportunities to publish the short story will thrive. Robert

Weaver's CBC radio programme, *Canadian Short Stories*, was widely credited with the beginnings of a national renaissance during the 1950s and 1960s.

In America, the short story is also still supported by the prestigious *New Yorker* magazine, which showcases short fiction from across the world, and by major awards for published short-story writers such as the Rea and O. Henry awards. The English and Scottish Arts Councils have backed a 'Save Our Short Stories' campaign which, amongst other things, is agitating for a similar prize in the UK. Its research confirms that British authors are unlikely to have a collection accepted by a mainstream publisher unless they are already well known as novelists.

But things are starting to change. The campaign has also discovered a rise in the number of anthologies appearing from both mainstream and independent presses. Small presses often compensate for the timidity of the big publishers, producing a large proportion of short-story collections. Weekend newspapers in Britain have begun to include short stories in review sections or as special supplements – mostly, it's true, in summer or at Christmas, but still another sign of a revival. Short stories are not an especially easy read. Because of their intensity, they can be quite demanding. But the age of text-messaging may well be disposed towards short concentrated bursts.

The Internet has played an enormous part in opening up new possibilities for authors worldwide. Writers and readers across the globe are able to exchange stories and to track down small publishers and magazines. Story sites are proliferating. On a mundane level it is cheaper and easier to publish online than it is to shift endless piles of books or magazines. Even more importantly, hypertext authors including Michael Joyce, Shelley Jackson and Robert Coover are working at the interface between the written word and the visual arts. While the death of the book has been greatly exaggerated, short snippets of prose are perfect for cyberspace. The very short story, such as those published on the McSweeney web site is coming into its own. The close relationship between visual imagery, photography, cinema and the short story is a recurring theme across this book. The new media offer writers a chance to take this affinity further, and to experiment with non-linear and multi-choice narratives.

There has never been a better time for writing short stories. Yet, while there are many excellent books on writing fiction and on creative writing generally, until recently there has been very little detailed material on the short story. This book is intended to meet the needs of both new and more experienced short-story writers, by demonstrating key techniques. Each chapter includes close readings of two or three core texts – some classic, some contemporary – along with references to other published stories. This close analysis is then followed up by practical activities to extend your own skills and stimulate fresh ideas. By completing the exercises, you will build up a portfolio of drafts and sketches ready for development into completed short stories.

The Indian writer R. K. Narayan has said that 'all theories of writing are bogus' (Narayan 1987: vii), and that every storyteller develops their own intuitive methods. To some extent, I agree. Writing is learnt by doing. No one can hand you step-by-step instructions for completing a decent short story as simply as baking a cake. But by showing you how other writers have handled structure, characterization, narrative voice, dialogue and other aspects of the craft, I hope to deepen the insights you learn from your own practice.

Narayan is just one of the many gifted writers who have been voracious readers – not just of short fiction or even novels, but of plays, poetry, anything they can lay their hands on. In itself, the short story is an enormously wide-ranging genre, and my first task is to introduce some of that diversity. Each chapter is based on an important subgenre, beginning with the yarn (including horror, tales of the supernatural and crime fiction) and moving on to consider image-based fiction, humorous writing, the fantastic, science fiction, realism and love stories. To get the most from the book, you need to read every chapter in sequence, attempting the activities. Even if you have no intention of ever writing a horror yarn, you can learn how to build suspense in any type of story by emulating Edgar Allan Poe. If, on the other hand, you are a horror fanatic, reading Katherine Mansfield or James Kelman might help you create interior monologues, evoking intense states of consciousness.

Many of the differences between writing short stories and writing a novel are related to questions of structure and pace. Approaching the short story through its subgenres will help you to explore different kinds of structure, from conventional plot-driven narrative to the more experimental. Within each chapter there should be something for everyone's taste. Besides, as the philosopher William James suggested, we could all benefit from breaking at least one habit a day. Why not start by writing something you've never tried before?

Of necessity, the categories are very broadly defined, often overlapping one another. Science fiction, fantasy and the yarn are intertwined, but there are separate strands. Since creative-writing teaching has tended to play down popular, plot-driven forms in favour of a 'literary' canon, I have given them each a chapter. As I show in Chapter 6, there are also close ties between the short story and journalism. Garrison Keillor is obviously a comic writer, deserving of his place in Chapter 3, but could equally well have featured in Chapter 6, as an example of social observation or of autobiographical and personal fiction.

One of the great strengths of the short-story form is this very ability to break generic boundaries. The distinctions between experimental and mainstream, or between literary and mass market, crumble in a technically adventurous piece such as Stephen King's 'That Feeling, You Can Only Say What it is in French' (King 2002). I hope the variety you encounter in my examples will encourage you to be inventive in your own writing. Most of the stories I mention are easily obtainable, many of them within recent anthologies. I have aimed for an eclectic choice, but inevitably, these samples reflect my own taste. They are not intended to represent an exhaustive survey.

The close readings within each chapter illustrate techniques and issues which are also relevant to other story genres. The opening chapter uses plot-driven stories, especially tales of the supernatural and crime fiction, to introduce the basics of the storyteller's art. Where do writers get their ideas from? How do you begin? How do you build up suspense and narrative drive? Chapter 2 turns to stories based on images, moods and impressions, looking especially at the epiphany, internal monologue and the 'stream of consciousness'. In Chapter 3 the emphasis is on humorous writing, including sketches, character-based comedy and parody, leading to a wider consideration of characterization and dialogue. We also explore what we mean by 'irony'. Chapter 4 focuses on fantasy and magic realism, also paying attention to viewpoint, multiple narration and the 'story within a story'. The work on science fiction and speculative fiction in Chapter 5 includes advice on writing strong beginnings. Chapter 6 groups together social observation and autobiographically based writing as forms of realism, suggesting ways of capturing memories and real-life experiences. It also discusses collections of linked stories or story cycles. Chapter 7 uses the concept of the love story as a narrative framework, along with some advice on adding passion to your writing. It concludes with suggestions for redrafting and editing.

My suggestions are intended as guidelines, not an infallible method. Bear in mind there are no hard and fast rules in writing; the greatest writers bend and break every convention. The activities have been designed for writers working alone, but may sometimes be adapted as workshop exercises. Some will work better for you than others. As so often in writing, you will learn through trial and error. So far as your own working habits are concerned, again you must find what suits you. I have typed even shopping lists since I was eight years old; others swear by longhand. I write first thing in the morning, others by night. I chisel the words out, sentence by sentence; others rush through an entire first draft, pruning back later. These differences are, in a sense, trivial. They are all a matter of temperament.

The book ends with a selection of resources for short-story writers, including outlets for publication. The short-story market is competitive, but nothing will develop your ability as much as the confidence you gain from seeing your work in print. Even if your stories are not accepted, sending them out into the world is a measure of the pride that you should feel. Nothing beats the sheer satisfaction of completing a story well told; or, as Raymond Carver puts it, in 'the swift leap of a good story, the excitement that often commences in the first sentence, the sense of beauty and mystery found in the best of them' (Carver 1998: xi).

Note on stories

All examples from published fiction are listed in the bibliography. Where a story is included in an anthology, the reference is to the anthology rather than the author's name. When stories are mentioned from more than one collection by the same author, the date is indicated in the text.

1

Spinning a yarn

Telling tales

'When I was a little kid my mother told me not to stare into the sun. So once, when I was six, I did.' Everyone likes a good story, and stories are everywhere – not just stories in books, and not just fictional stories, but stories on the news, in songs and in jokes. We also love telling tales, often tales about ourselves. The passage I've just quoted is an example. I haven't taken it from a short story but from a film, Darren Aronofsky's cult movie, *Pi*. Used in the opening voice-over, these two simple sentences hook the audience into the story, making them want to know what happened next.

Look at those lines again. This story could go anywhere, leading into an extended memoir about being six years old; or, as another possibility, turning into a science-fiction story if staring at the sun is just a part of the character's fascination with the solar system. We have not yet got to know this character. But he or she has spoken directly to us, establishing a compelling narrative voice. S/he is spinning a yarn.

'Narrative' shapes experience; it orders life into a sequence of events. Neuroscientist Antonio Damasio believes that narrative is a human instinct, and that we are telling ourselves wordless stories before we even start to speak (Damasio 2000: 188–9). Paul Broks claims that 'a human being is a story-telling machine. The self is a story' (Broks 2003: 41).

9

You can't turn off that machine. Tittle-tattle is as old as talk itself, and though no one likes a snitch we can't resist telling tales. Iona and Peter Opie collected dozens of playground rhymes from up and down the British Isles, all aimed at 'tell tale tits', the most popular version dating back at least two hundred years. In the fairy story 'Rumpelstiltskin', the wicked gnome even tells tales on himself. Confident that the Queen will not guess his name, and therefore she will have to keep her bargain by giving him her child, he prances about in the forest singing:

> Merrily the feast I'll make,
> To-day I'll brew, to-morrow bake;
> Merrily I'll dance and sing,
> For next day will a stranger bring:
> Little does my lady dream
> Rumpel-Stilts-Kin is my name!
>
> (Opie 1974: 197)

Stories are repeated, passed on and transformed. The many folk tales which have survived testify to the power of the oral tradition. West African culture contains numerous trickster tales, featuring Anansi, who is sometimes a spider, sometimes a turtle, a coyote or even a poor farmer. Whatever shape he takes, his character's always the same. Like Br'er Rabbit in the *Uncle Remus* stories, he always outwits those who think they're smarter than he is. Another humble character who ends up on top is the poor boy Aladdin, star of countless Christmas pantomimes. 'Aladdin and the Enchanted Lamp' belongs to a great compendium of stories from India, Persia and the Arab world called *The Thousand and One Nights*, which also includes 'Sindbad the Sailor.' Some of Sindbad's voyages in *The Thousand and One Nights* echo Homer's *Odyssey*, either because both the Greek writer and the Arabian writer had heard the same seafaring yarns or because the tales about Odysseus had themselves crossed the ocean. The *Odyssey* still inspires all kinds of different texts, from James Joyce's novel *Ulysses* to the film *O Brother, Where Art Thou?*

The first printed version of *The Thousand and One Nights* has been dated to the ninth century AD, but the tales themselves are much older. Just as they were worked and reworked by professional storytellers so the printed versions have taken on many forms and many voices, from the street language of Cairo to Victorian English, censored for family reading. The Prologue to the tales provides a framework to the collection through the story of King Shahriyar who makes a custom of marrying a virgin each night and killing her in the morning. The habit is broken by Shahrazad, who stays alive by telling stories; if Shahriyar has her executed, he'll never hear the rest. Shahrazad, the bride whose tales are so irresistible, stands for the magic of storytelling. She embodies the idea of narrative drive – the urge to know what happens next.

Plot

But what makes a good yarn? How do you weave the spell? If anyone knows the answer, it should be Stephen King. He is one of the most popular yarn-spinners around. Michael Chabon, the editor of *McSweeney's Mammoth Treasury of Thrilling Tales*, calls him 'the Last Master of the Plotted Short Story' (Chabon 2003: 7). Thinking up a clever plot, a real page-turner, might seem the place to start. Yet King warns aspiring writers away from conscious plotting: 'Plot is, I think, the good writer's last resort and the dullard's first choice' (King 2001: 189). He says plots are artificial, while stories are organisms, which grow out of situations and characters. If you impose a preordained plot, you're restricting that imaginative growth, and the result is unlikely to convince your readers. King strips storytelling down to three basic elements: 'In my view, stories and novels consist of three parts: narration, which moves the story from point A to point B and finally to point Z; description, which creates a sensory reality for the reader; and dialogue, which brings characters to life through speech' (King 2001: 187).

King's own methods are based on intuition, on recognizing a possibility and on following through. He places his characters in a predicament, for instance in a room from which there seems to be no escape. 'In the Death Room' places an unarmed political prisoner in a torture chamber, while the character in '1408' is trapped by a haunted hotel room. A simple idea or an image can generate numerous possibilities. 'L. T.'s Theory of Pets' was born from the observation that pets sometimes imprint not on their owner, but on their partner, and that this comes to symbolize the breakdown of a marriage. 'Everything's Eventual' was sparked off by the mental image of someone tipping small change into the gutter. In all of these stories the writer is wondering what would happen if something, great or small, changed in the lives of his characters. King's own curiosity transmits itself to the reader, as he speculates on the likely consequences.

So writing a successful yarn doesn't start with a fully formed plot, like pulling rabbits out of a hat. It isn't about outsmarting the reader – or at least I don't think so because, as I said in my introduction, there are no rules in writing. King advises every writer to read as much as they can, to learn by example, and I can only recommend that you follow his advice. In this chapter, we're going to look at a range of different yarns, paying special attention to two classic tales by Edgar Allan Poe and Arthur Conan Doyle. By 'yarn' I mean the type of story it is often hardest to put down – a story full of adventure and suspense, the kind of story that is sometimes described as 'plot-driven' and deserves to be called a 'thrilling tale'. This is a very large category, covering horror fiction, suspense, tales of the supernatural, crime-writing, travellers' tales, war stories, animal tales. It also embraces science fiction and fantasy, which will later have chapters to themselves. Even if you are not a regular reader of such tales, the process of studying and experimenting with plot-based forms will develop an awareness of narrative drive that can feed into your writing.

Creating suspense: 'The Fall of the House of Usher' (Edgar Allan Poe, 1840)

Edgar Allan Poe opens his best-known horror story by conjuring up a sense of foreboding:

> During the whole of a dull, dark, and soundless day in the autumn of the year, when the clouds hung oppressively low in the heavens, I had been passing alone, on horseback, through a singularly dreary tract of country; and at length found myself, as the shades of the evening drew on, within view of the melancholy House of Usher.
>
> (Poe 1994: 76)

These long, meandering sentences are in a totally different style to the voice-over from *Pi*, with which I began this chapter. But, in their different ways, both excerpts speak directly to the reader, with a forceful narrative voice. In each case, a first-person narrator has something urgent to tell you, something to make you sit up and listen, just like Shahriyar when Shahrazad wove her spell.

The narrator relives his experiences through a detailed description of landscape and weather. This is the 'sensory reality' mentioned by King as one of the three essential components of narrative fiction. Poe specializes in piling sensation on sensation, immersing the reader in his nightmarish vision. Even the sound of the words ('dull, dark, and soundless') adds to the gloom. When the narrator reaches the house itself, the atmosphere deepens. Pausing to ask himself why the decaying mansion induces such 'an utter depression of soul', he can only put it down to 'a mystery all insoluble' (Poe 1994: 76). The attempt to explain this mystery sets the story in motion, taking it, in King's words, 'from point A to point B and finally to point Z'. Already, on the first page, we are feeling nervous. We know something nasty is going to happen.

Poe prolongs the suspense, gradually revealing the secrets behind those 'vacant and eye-like windows'. By lingering on details, he builds up anticipation while also increasing the emotional effect on the reader. A later writer, H. P. Lovecraft, emphasizes the importance of this imaginative impact in horror fiction: 'Atmosphere is the all-important thing, for the final criterion of authenticity is not the dovetailing of a plot but the creation of a given sensation' (Lovecraft 1998: 57).

Here, the plot turns upon the basic notion of a 'skeleton in the closet' – a family secret, uncovered by an outsider. Visiting his old friend, Roderick Usher, the narrator finds him morbidly hypersensitive, while his twin sister Madeline seems to be in terminal decline, and is eventually laid to rest in the family vault. They are the last of their line; their condition is mirrored by the physical deterioration of the house itself. The horror reaches its climax in a final 'twist', involving one of Poe's favourite motifs, the premature burial: '*We have put her living in the tomb!*' (Poe 1994: 94).

Poe uses familiar themes, such as the unusually close bond between twins; he also exploits common fears, such as the dread of being buried alive. (In fact this anxiety was so widespread during the nineteenth century there was even a Society for the Prevention of People Being Buried Alive.) These elements are far more important than the bare mechanics of plot.

In Poe's story, the narrator has a desperate need to share his terrible experiences and to convince us of their reality. This emotional intensity adds power to the narrative. Every tale has a teller, in addition to the author, the person who wrote the piece. This is obvious in a first-person narrative like 'The Fall of the House of Usher' where, though we know little about the 'I' character, his personality colours the entire story. Sustaining a strong narrative voice is essential to all storytelling. Here the emotional intensity of that voice drives the narrative towards its grand finale. The 'dead' Madeline rises from the tomb, only to expire with her brother. As the narrator flees the moonlit mansion, the house splits in two: 'My brain reeled as I saw the mighty walls rushing asunder – there was a long tumultuous shouting sound like the voice of a thousand waters – and the deep and dank tarn at my feet closed suddenly and silently over the fragments of the "HOUSE OF USHER" ' (Poe 1994: 95).

End of story. While there are always ambiguities in any tale of mystery and suspense, one thing we know for sure; this is the final sentence. It ends with a bang. Mysteries are solved; there is plot resolution. Horror stories tap into our deepest fears, about death, decay and suffering, yet they are also hugely enjoyable. One of the reasons for this is the sheer pleasure of narrative. Like any good yarn, a horror story offers a clear dramatic structure with a beginning that whets the appetite and a resounding conclusion.

While we're reading horror fiction, we are in a world of make-believe, which on one level is very real, but at the same time is at a safe distance. King explains this succinctly when, in his story 'Everything's Eventual', he differentiates between 'TV-scared' and 'real-scared' (King 2002: 251). In 'The Fall of the House of Usher', Poe's overblown language and melodramatic endings remind us that we're in a fantasy. King's short stories are more realistic in style, but he often counteracts the disturbing elements by granting us a happy ending. For instance, in his update of the 'premature burial' theme, 'Autopsy Room Four' (King 2002), his narrator is fully conscious but unable to move as medical staff prepare to dissect his supposed corpse. The experience is made horribly vivid, and all too plausible, as the narrator listens to them joking, playing loud music and flirting with each other. Then, at the very last minute, someone bursts through the door to save him. Like much horror literature and film, for instance the *Scream* series, King's work also keeps the ultimate terrors at bay by using humour. His narrator reflects sardonically on his predicament, even giving the staff nicknames.

Horror fiction enables us to test our own limits, dabbling with our deepest fears and sometimes confronting realities too unbearable to contemplate in true-to-life fashion. Gala Blau's 'Outfangthief' (Jones 2002) was inspired by an article in the British newspaper, the *Guardian*, concerning apotemnophilia, the removal of limbs for sexual gratification. The original article concerned the death of a 'patient' during one of these voluntary amputations. Blau's changed the fetish to acrotomophilia, the desire to have sex with amputees. Deeply in debt and with a nubile daughter to protect, Blau's protagonist is on the run from a vicious criminal when she finds sanctuary with a colony of vampires. By most standards, these supernatural predators are terrifying, yet they seem preferable to the monsters at large in the real world as the villain's perverted designs are revealed. A very grisly tale indeed, 'Outfangthief' is the only truly disturbing story amongst the examples in this chapter.

Tall tales

'Autopsy Room Four' is an example of what we might call the 'tall tale'. One-paragraph newspaper stories are often based on tall tales – this one, for instance, discovered just as I was reading 'Autopsy Room Four':

> **'Dead man' died at his own wake**
>
> A FATHER died at his own wake after a blunder by medical staff. Carlos Valencia was certified dead at a clinic. But when he was taken home for his wake, his daughter – a nurse – realized he still had a pulse. She called an ambulance but, by the time it arrived, her 94-year-old father was dead. A doctor said: 'Neither a doctor nor the funeral director realized he was still alive. That is really incredible.' The family is now suing the clinic in Buenos Aires.
>
> (*Metro*, 11 September 2003)

By calling this piece a 'tall tale' I don't mean to imply it's untrue, just that it beggars belief. It is 'strange but true'. In the British *Sunday Times* half a dozen or so such stories are gathered together under the heading 'This Life'. A drunk driver pretends to be the Pope, claiming 'spiritual immunity'; an ordinary office clerk turns into a masked superhero after work, cutting free clamped vehicles in the role of 'Angle-Grinder Man'. Nearly all these stories are alleged to have taken place somewhere far away; I was reading the Buenos Aires story in England, but it was supposed to have happened in South America. Urban myths circulate mostly by word of mouth, though their origins may be in obscure publications. The Ship of Fools web site traces the 'Drilling to Hell' story in Californian radio stations and Scandinavian missionary news-sheets, but ultimately it is difficult to locate the myth in a single point of origin. According to this urban legend, Russian scientists drilling into the earth heard the screams

15

of the damned. They had penetrated Hell. In some versions they had even seen a pillar of light shaping itself into a bat-like creature, and spelling out the words 'I have conquered'. Other more plausible myths concern the frozen urine supposedly dropped from passing planes or the HIV sufferer who sets about deliberately infecting strangers. 'Drilling to Hell' is reminiscent of Arthur Conan Doyle's novel *When the World Screamed*, and urban myths also feed into contemporary fiction, for instance Neil Gaiman's 'Closing Time':

> Then Paul told us a true story about a friend of his who had picked up a hitchhiker, and dropped her off at a place she said was her house, and when he went back the next morning, it turned out to be a cemetery. I mentioned that exactly the same thing had happened to a friend of mine as well. Martyn said that it had not only happened to a friend of his, but, because the hitchhiking girl looked so cold, the friend had lent her his coat, and the next morning, in the cemetery, he found his coat all neatly folded on her grave.
>
> Martyn went and got another round of drinks, and we wondered why all these ghost-women were zooming round the country all night and hitchhiking home, and Martyn said that probably living hitchhikers these days were the exception, not the rule.
>
> (Chabon 2003: 146)

One of the most famous literary tall tales is that of Rip Van Winkle, whose adventures are recounted in Washington Irving's *Sketch Book* from 1819. Rip Van Winkle falls asleep for twenty years after a drinking session, waking up to find the world around him changed completely. Travellers' tales and seafaring yarns always stretch credibility. Jim Shepard's 'Tedford and the Megalodon' evokes an Antarctic sea monster, while in H. P. Lovecraft's 'Dagon' a shipwrecked sailor is washed up in an undersea realm. Reading Glen David Gold's 'The Tears of Squonk, and What Happened Thereafter' (Chabon 2003), you may well believe that once upon a time in Tennessee they hanged an elephant for murder. Gold's account is as shocking and as moving as George Orwell's famous essay, 'Shooting an Elephant'. Credulity is stretched to the limit when proof emerges of an actual elephant conspiracy, but Gold's references to photographic and eyewitness accounts keep up the appearance of historical reliability.

Tall tales aim to persuade the reader that the incredible really can happen. They often are tongue-in-cheek. But a really skilful writer can make the most ridiculous tale seem plausible and even rather chilling. In Poppy Z. Brite's 'O Death, Where is Thy Spatula?' (Jones 2002), her narrator, Dr Brite, a New Orleans coroner, raises her favourite chef from the dead so that she can continue to enjoy such delights as 'a disc of beef marrow melting into a fricassee of chanterelles, its flavor brightened by a persillade so finely chopped you could barely see it' (Jones 2002: 179).

This story begins in a chatty, down-to-earth style: 'The main thing you need to know about me is that I love eating more than anything else in the world. More than sex, more than tropical vacations, more than reading, more than any drug I've ever tried' (Jones 2002: 174–5). Dr Brite goes on to discuss eating, restaurants and, most of all, the food cooked by the great Devlin Lemon. Like 'The Fall of the House of Usher', this story seduces the reader with sensuous description. When Dr Brite switches to the autopsy room, the description is equally full, but this time with the grim medical details of a fatal gunshot wound. Gradually she realizes that the corpse she is about to dissect is none other than Devlin Lemon.

This story is very well researched, and its author's knowledgability adds conviction. She knows how a bullet enters the brain and how rigor mortis affects a body. Herself married to a chef, she knows they often have a wedding band tattooed on the finger instead of wearing a ring. The story is three quarters through before Dr Brite tells the reader what she decides to do with Devlin's corpse, and then very indirectly.

The author also makes the most of the New Orleans setting, especially the voodoo connection when, posing as a writer researching a story, Dr Brite visits a Haitian herbalist. What she learns there is very convincingly matched with her medical knowledge. The illegal plant required for a voodoo resurrection can be broken down into its chemical elements – 'atropine', 'hyoscyamine', 'scopolamine': 'Atropine is the active ingredient in Lomotil, which is used to control severe diarrhea. Hyoscyamine is used in Cystospaz and Uriced, which are used for glaucoma, urinary obstructions, and bowel problems' (Jones 2002: 183).

It all sounds impressive. The process of restoring Devlin to life is described meticulously, including the moment when Dr Brite contributes her own finger bone to the potion. Poppy Z. Brite has made the story believable by anchoring it in everyday life and in scientific detail.

Games and puzzles: 'The Red-Headed League' (Arthur Conan Doyle, 1892)

Whether you write horror stories or any other kind of fiction, you are licensed to daydream. Freud once commented that 'every child at play behaves like a creative writer, in that he creates a world of his own or, rather, he rearranges the things of his world in a new way' (Freud 1990: 131–2). Looking back on her own childhood, the Canadian author Alice Munro relates reading and writing to this world of play:

> The worlds contained in books were so marvellous to me that I just had to do more of that myself. At first it was reading and living in imagination in things that other people had written, and then after a while that didn't satisfy me any longer and I had to be living in the thing that I myself made up.
>
> (Miller 1984: 123)

Robert Louis Stevenson also relates his development as a writer to childhood make-believe: 'Men are born with various manias: from my earliest childhood, it was mine to make a plaything of imaginary series of events; and as soon as I was able to write, I became a good friend to the paper-makers' (Stevenson 1920: 116).

The Brontë children turned the games they played with toy soldiers into a series of intricate booklets, practising storytelling skills that would produce *Wuthering Heights* and *Jane Eyre*. Writing lets you take charge of your fantasy world and pretend to be somebody else. Poppy Z. Brite names the New Orleans coroner after herself. You could say she's playing at doctors.

While Poe, Brite and King use mystery and suspense for emotional effect, classic detective fiction constructs a mental puzzle, like a chess game or crossword puzzle. Mystery in a Sherlock Holmes story does not depend on 'dream-like' qualities, visceral reactions or ambiguous states of consciousness. This is a world that is highly controlled, as we can see in 'The Red-Headed League'. Unlike Poe, Conan Doyle wastes no time establishing an atmosphere. His narrator, Dr Watson, sticks strictly to the facts:

> I had called upon my friend, Mr Sherlock Holmes, one day in the autumn of last year, and found him in deep conversation with a

very stout, florid-faced elderly gentleman, with fiery red hair. With an apology for my intrusion, I was about to withdraw, when Holmes pulled me abruptly into the room, and closed the door behind me.

(Conan Doyle 1994: 29)

Watson specifies 'one day in the autumn of last year'; we don't need to know if it was 'dull, dark, and soundless' like that autumn day in Poe's tale. He concentrates on the 'very stout, florid-faced elderly gentleman, with fiery red hair', because the gentleman's physical appearance relates to the unfolding mystery. Whenever Watson furnishes a description, we suspect we're being handed a clue. He isn't wallowing in mood or atmosphere, but is carefully reconstructing the circumstances surrounding a particular case. Watson aims for objective observation, while Poe's narrator monitors his own emotional state – 'an utter depression of soul which I can compare to no earthly sensation more properly than to the after-dream of the reveller upon opium – the bitter lapse into everyday life – the hideous dropping off of the veil' (Poe 1994: 76). Watson sometimes refers to his feelings, but he never dwells on them. Crouching in the darkness with his pistol cocked, near the climax of the story, he notes 'something depressing and subduing in the sudden gloom, and in the cold, dank air of the vault' (Conan Doyle 1994: 51), but this is a perfectly normal response, sketched in to complete his impressions.

Although the opening paragraphs of 'The Fall of the House of Usher' and 'The Red-Headed League' are so very different, both of these classic yarns build up suspense by withholding and releasing information. Watson's narrative appears direct and factual, but there are pages of delay before we discover anything about the nature of the case itself. Events are largely revealed through dialogue, in conversations or first-hand testimony. Early on in 'The Red-Headed League', Holmes's speeches build up anticipation by teasing the reader, referring obliquely to the case in question:

You have heard me remark that the strangest and most unique things are very often connected not with the larger but with the smaller crimes, and occasionally, indeed, where there is room for doubt whether any positive crime has been committed. As far as I have heard, it is impossible for me to say whether the present case is an instance of crime or not, but the course of events is certainly among the most singular that I have ever listened to.

(Conan Doyle 1994: 30)

Having made these opening remarks at some length, Holmes displays his well-known powers of observation on the red-headed client: 'Beyond the obvious facts that he has at some time done manual labour, that he takes snuff, that he is a Freemason, that he has been in China, and that he has done a considerable amount of writing lately, I can deduce nothing else' (Conan Doyle 1994: 31). These 'obvious facts' have, of course, escaped Watson, whose own quick appraisal precedes this analysis. Finally, when Holmes has explained his reasoning, his client, Jabez Wilson, takes the floor, repeating his predicament for Watson's benefit.

This use of dialogue, embedding a 'story within a story' is a very common device in the old-fashioned yarn. In 'The Fall of the House of Usher', the narrator summarizes conversations he has had with Roderick Usher, in which Usher has described his plight at some length. In 'The Red-Headed League', Watson gives a verbatim account of the conversations which make up so much of the narrative. His powers of recall seem almost as astounding as Holmes's powers of perception. But while such feats of memory may seem implausible, the retelling of conversations is something we all do, and a passage like the one below sounds like ordinary chatter. Wilson runs a small pawnbroker's shop. After answering a newspaper advertisement by a charitable foundation, the Red-Headed League, he has taken a job writing out passages from the *Encyclopaedia Britannica*. Arriving at work one day, he finds the League has shut up shop:

'I was staggered, sir. I did not know what to do. Then I called at the offices round, but none of them seemed to know anything about it. Finally, I went to the landlord, who is an accountant living on the ground floor, and I asked him if he could tell me what had become of the Red-headed League. He said that he had never heard of any such body. Then I asked him who Mr Duncan Ross was. He answered that the name was new to him.

' "Well," said I, "the gentleman at No.4."

' "What, the red-headed man?"

' "Yes."

' "Oh," said he, "his name was William Morris. He was a solicitor, and was using my room as a temporary convenience until his new premises were ready. He moved out yesterday." '

(Conan Doyle 1994: 40–1)

More recent writers such as Ruth Rendell also dramatize the work of detection through elaborate question-and-answer sessions. Her policemen, Wexford and Burden, follow in the footsteps of Holmes and Watson. They are also contrasting personalities. Wexford has the sharper intellect, while Burden, like Watson, is slightly naïve. The interplay between the characters spices up passages of factual information. In Rendell's story, 'Means of Evil', different types of deadly mushroom are discussed in painstaking detail, a process made much livelier by the competitive sparring between the Chief Inspector and his subordinate.

Conan Doyle's stories provide the prototype for the classic detective story and the figure of the detective who solves the crime through superior logic. The characteristics we associate with Holmes are keen observation, quick-wittedness and rationalism. However, these traits are qualified by an introspective side. When the great detective takes time off to go to a concert, this other side comes to the fore: 'All the afternoon he sat in the stalls wrapped in the most perfect happiness, gently waving his long thin fingers in time to the music, while his gently smiling face and his languid, dreamy eyes were as unlike those of Holmes the sleuth-hound, Holmes the relentless, keen-witted, ready-handed criminal agent, as it was possible to conceive' (Conan Doyle 1994: 45). But the violin-playing aesthete is essential to the other half of his nature. At some stage in every case, Holmes withdraws into himself in order to make the intuitive leap which solves the mystery. Here, it is the possibility that the Red-Headed League is simply a diversion to get Wilson out of his office. Once this breakthrough has been made, Holmes discerns a pattern linking seemingly random events. A complex plot is uncovered, based on the digging of an underground tunnel from Wilson's office to a bank vault beneath the City of London.

Conan Doyle turned out his Sherlock Holmes stories quickly, to satisfy his vast readership. He worked backwards from an ending which was already clear in his mind. Nonetheless, the ideas themselves came out of the blue, often when he was doing something physical such as playing cricket. Ruth Rendell also thinks up her stories while she's out walking or exercising on her treadmill. Many crime writers insist on planning ahead. Martin Edwards says 'there is no room for slippage in short story writing ... So you need a tightly constructed plot, and that in turn means that you must plan where your story is going' (*Writing Magazine* February–March 1997). But most, like Holmes himself, rely to some degree on instinct.

Structure

As we can see in 'The Red-Headed League', plot needs to be handled differently in crime fiction, because you're trying to lay clues for the reader. In 'The Fall of the House of Usher', horror is piled upon horror, until the final nightmare is unleashed. Both tales rely on suspense and on gradually releasing crucial information. But one is structured by logic, the other by sensation.

Stories which seem cleverly plotted are often carefully structured. By 'structure', I mean the order in which you place the events. Structure shapes the raw material. It provides a pattern which gives meaning to the story. Looking once more at 'The Fall of the House of Usher', we can reduce its basic components to the concept of an ordeal which is foreshadowed at the very start and which then progressively worsens. This structure is followed by many other tales of the supernatural, such as those by M. R. James, H. P. Lovecraft, Edith Wharton and Ramsey Campbell. In Henry James's 'The Turn of the Screw', a governess senses that her charges are being manipulated by malicious ghosts. As her fears intensify, the evil presence is manifest. But we also suspect that she herself is unhinged, projecting these influences from her own distorted mind.

Detective fiction puts together the events of the crime (A) with another string of events, the investigation (B). At the end, the detective has reconstructed that first story. A murder mystery like Rendell's 'Means of Evil' can be said to begin at the end of Story A, with the death. Wexford and Burden then work backwards from that point until the story is complete. This may remind you of Conan Doyle's working methods.

In 'The Red-Headed League', A and B run in parallel, with the crime apprehended as the investigation ends. Holmes, as always, solves the case through deduction. He explains that 'the more bizarre a thing is the less mysterious it proves to be' (Conan Doyle 1994: 42–3). In other words, the most baffling details will provide the answers. The most bizarre aspect of this story is Wilson's job with the League. Why on earth would you be paid to copy out the encyclopaedia just because you have red hair?

Slightly less strange, but still rather unusual, is the behaviour of Wilson's assistant, Spaulding. Not many pawnbroker's assistants would work at half the normal wage. Wilson has not given this point very much thought, nor questioned Spaulding's eagerness to develop photographs in his cellar. It was, of course, Spaulding who pointed out the League's advertisement. Once Holmes has deduced that Spaulding is tunnelling while Wilson is out of the way, a process of elimination leads him to the probable target and to Saturday night as the best time for the break-in. He is then able to catch the criminals red-handed.

Clues are laid precisely. Major clues are supplied by the 'bizarre', minor ones often by the detective's actions. Most readers will share Watson's incomprehension when Holmes finds a pretext to look at Spaulding's trousers. His motive becomes obvious once the connection with tunnelling is clear. The Sherlock Holmes stories are packed with clues, red herrings and incidental detail, such as the false address that turns out to be a 'manufactory of artificial kneecaps' (Conan Doyle 1994: 41). Because they are so densely written, the stories demand a certain amount of concentration. Holmes's many fans soon find themselves caught up in a world of their own. Perhaps this is why Holmes remains such a popular figure, his adventures dramatized on film, TV and radio, and his character reworked by modern authors.

Detective stories, tales of the supernatural and other types of traditional yarn are structured according to obvious rules, which you can follow with relative ease. But structure matters even when the scaffolding is less clearly visible. The stories in this chapter are 'plot-driven', structured by a chain of external events, leading towards a satisfactory conclusion. As we shall see in Chapter 2, this is not the only way to structure a short story. While plot-driven fiction ties up the loose ends and delivers solutions, other types of short story thrive on the mysterious and inconsequential, capturing thoughts and impressions. In these stories, structure is based on patterns of language and imagery. Even the 'stream of consciousness' narratives by writers such as James Kelman only appear to be ordered at random. They are just as carefully structured as the traditional 'yarn'.

Unlike style or plot or characters, structure is something you can borrow wholesale, using another writer's story as a template for your own. You can fit your material into structures used by Conan Doyle or Poe, while still developing your own distinctive voice. In Chapter 7, I examine structure and pace in a story by Chekhov, tracing narrative patterns which you might also adapt to your own work. Finding the right structure often takes time, evolving alongside aspects of style. Occasionally you might want to map out a structure in advance as an experiment, like my story 'Twentieth Frame', conceived as a sequence of snapshots (see Chapter 2). But even then form and content are closely integrated, each reflecting the other. The structures you have borrowed will soon become your own.

Writing in the dark

So where to begin? How do you start putting words down on paper? Let me quote from Margaret Atwood: 'Where is the story? The story is in the dark. That is why inspiration is thought of as coming in flashes. Going into a narrative – into the narrative process – is a dark road. You can't see your way ahead' (Atwood 2002: 176). You're an explorer, travelling without a map, searching out the story, as King puts it, 'like fossils in the ground' (King 2001: 188). You're taking a leap in the dark in another sense, in that if you want to make an impact on the reader you must be willing to visit the dark places in yourself. Poe harnesses primitive fears about madness, incarceration and death. King's 'The Man in the Black Suit' summons up childhood terrors that most of us banish in our waking lives.

Desperate for money, Robert Louis Stevenson racked his brains for a plot. He couldn't think of anything until he dreamt a few scenes which generated 'The Strange Case of Dr Jekyll and Mr Hyde'. Stevenson set great store by the 'unseen collaborators who did half the writer's work while he was asleep and probably continued when he thought he was managing all by himself:

> They share plainly in his training; they have plainly learned like him to build the scheme of a considerate story and to arrange emotions in progressive order; only I think they have more talent; and one thing is beyond doubt, they can tell him a story piece by piece, like a serial, and keep him all the while in ignorance of where they aim.

> (Stevenson 1950: 164)

Many other writers, including Graham Greene, William Burroughs, Franz Kafka and Doris Lessing testify to the importance of dreaming in the creative process. Some keep a dream diary. The British novelist Nicholas Royle collected some of these writers' dreams for his anthology, *The Tiger Garden*.

Few stories are wholly original. The premature burial has been used again and again. Conan Doyle exploited many other ideas first seen in Poe, for instance the central concept of 'The Purloined Letter' which he incorporated into 'A Scandal in Bohemia'. Reworking other writers' ideas is fine, so long as you're adapting those ideas, not just copying someone else's work. Stephen King acknowledges his debt to Nathaniel Hawthorne in his afterword to 'The Man in the Black Suit' (King 2002: 62–3).

But you do have to make the old stories new. You have to bring your tales to life. In order to do this, you have to explore language. You may decide to luxuriate in descriptive passages like Poe, or to use a plainer, fast-moving style like Conan Doyle's. Either way, you're making the story your own. You are the storyteller. You are Shahrazad, weaving magic out of words.

Activity 1   Beginning, Middle and End

Once there was an ugly duckling. He was miserable because the other ducklings laughed at him. One day, he woke up to find his dingy grey feathers had turned snowy white. He wasn't an ugly duckling after all. He'd grown up into a beautiful swan, the loveliest bird on the lake.

This is a version of Hans Christian Andersen's 'The Ugly Duckling', a story which you may know even if you haven't read it. I've reduced it to five sentences; could you condense it further? Think of another well-known story, and see if you can tell it in four sentences or even three – a beginning, middle and end.

In 'The Ugly Duckling', as in most stories, there is a process of change. Something is different by the end, even if events are not as dramatic as the duckling's transformation.

Activity 2   'Once there was . . .'

Write a sentence beginning, 'Once there was . . .' What happens next? Complete your story in four sentences.

The film director Jean-Luc Godard said that films have to have a beginning, a middle and an end, but not necessarily in that order. The same is true of all storytelling. In the previous exercise, you worked on a linear narrative, reconstructing a chain of events chronologically. What would happen if you changed the order? Supposing you began the ugly duckling story with the third sentence?

I've told the ugly duckling's story from his point of view – not as it might be seen from the perspective, for instance, of the other ducks who mocked him. In stripping down this simple story to the bare bones, I've missed out a lot of elements, besides plot, that make fiction come to life – characterization, atmosphere, the sound of the language. In choosing the 'once there was' format we all know from fairy tales, I've cut down the choices writers have to make about who is telling a story, from which perspective, and from which point in time.

You now have the rough draft of a story – a beginning, middle and end, though you may not necessarily want to tell them in sequence. Working as quickly as you can, complete your story in a thousand words.

Activity 3   The ultimate horror

'The Fall of the House of Usher' is one of several Poe stories expressing a fear of premature burial. In his time, being buried alive was considered a real possibility, but it can also be regarded a form of claustrophobia, an irrational terror, like the fear of snakes or spiders.

What's your ultimate horror? Is there something that you can't bear to touch? Or a sound that sets you on edge? If you're afraid of heights, imagine being stuck at the edge of a cliff. Describe whatever it is that repels you in as much physical detail as you can manage. What is it about spiders that is so repugnant? What do you see when you peer into the void?

Remember waking up from a nightmare? Write down what was so frightening – even if you can't remember it all. You may have a recurring dream. I often dream that I've moved house. I realize I've made a terrible mistake, that I was happy where I was and have lost my home forever.

Use your phobia or nightmare as the beginning of a story. Writing in the first person, imagine what has brought you to this point, in the worst of all worlds. Are you going to escape or are you trapped by this, the ultimate terror? The point is not to analyse your fear, but to describe it. Both this exercise and the next one develop a sense of narrative drive. In the next section, I am going to show how these images can be developed into a narrative based on the 'sensation' structure I found in Poe's writing. The lessons you will learn in plot construction can be applied to all kinds of storytelling, not just horror fiction.

Activity 4   Things that go bump in the night

'There is the touch on the shoulder that comes when you are walking quickly homewards in the dark hours, full of anticipation of the warm room and bright fire, and when you pull up, startled, what face or no-face do you see?' (James 1993: 645–6). M. R. James is talking about all those creepy moments that, like Stevenson's nightmare, form the seeds of a story. Spooks, monsters and bogeymen are never far away. The vampire, the werewolf, the zombie and the creature from the deep or from outer space – they all spring back to life in different forms, as they are reinvented for each new generation. Forget what you've read or seen before. Light some candles and sketch out a few ideas, using the scenarios I've set out below. Write as quickly as you can. There is no need, at this stage, to fill out the whole story.

The chase

Something is after you – man, beast or monster. You could be running down a street, through a forest or a jungle. Or perhaps you are inside and the thing is out there, coming to get you.

Shape-changers

The werewolf is just one example of a human being turning into an animal. Think of other possibilities. What would it feel like inside the skin of the beast? Without ever using the term, Ursula Le Guin's 'The Wife's Story' reverses the transformation from man into 'werewolf', so that it's the man who seems unnatural while the wolf is entirely normal.

The Double

What if another side of your self suddenly came to life? Stevenson's 'The Strange Case of Dr Jekyll and Mr Hyde' is the best-known example of a divided personality. Poe's 'William Wilson' also brings its narrator face to face with his alter ego, while in Henry James's 'The Jolly Corner' the protagonist is haunted by the person he might have been, if he had stayed at home in New York instead of moving to Europe.

Pandora's Box

According to the legend, the gods gave Pandora a mysterious box which she was forbidden to open. Of course, she disobeyed, and evil, in its multiple forms, flew out into the world. In Lovecraft's 'The Statement of Randolph Carter', a man excavating a tomb is annihilated by something beyond all powers of description: '*Great God! I never dreamed of THIS!*' (Lovecraft 1999: 11). The Pandora's box story is based on two concepts – the idea of curiosity getting the better of you and the notion of a deadly object, which could be a closed box or a sealed tomb, or the library book in M. R. James's 'The Tractate Middoth'. James himself said 'Many common objects may be made the vehicles of retribution, and where retribution is not called for, of malice' (James 1993: 646). Invent your own deadly object or mysterious package as the basis for a story.

Haunted

Sometimes ghosts get out and about, like the headless horseman in Washington Irving's 'The Legend of Sleepy Hollow'. But they very often stay indoors, associated with a particular place. In both Edith Wharton's 'Kerfol' and Elizabeth Bowen's 'The Cat Jumps', a new tenant encounters weird goings-on in their home. Wharton's house is the traditional castle, while Bowen's is much more ordinary. Ghosts are everywhere. Find your haunted space, and they will follow.

Choosing one of the sketches you have written here or in Exercise 3, borrow the 'sensation' structure used in 'The Fall of the House of Usher' to complete a short story. Like Poe, write through a first-person narrator, and crank up the horror stage by stage. The original exercise will provide the horrific climax, like Madeline's emergence from the tomb. Unless you're playing it for laughs, avoid explicit violence. In Lovecraft's 'The Picture in the House', the image of blood dripping onto the page suggests the unspeakable horrors in the upstairs room far more effectively than any literal description.

Activity 5   Looking for clues

As we saw in 'The Red-Headed League', classic detective fiction is assembled from a series of clues. In finding the connection between incidental details, the detective solves the mystery. A mobile phone provides the crucial evidence in Ian Rankin's 'Tell Me who to Kill' (Edwards 2003). The title comes from a text message on a mobile phone found by the roadside. Before reading the story, jot down a few ideas for a story based on this image. What was the phone doing there? Who was the message for, and what was its purpose? Then read the story. You will be surprised by Rankin's solution. Once you've reached the end, go back over this story, looking for other clues, for instance, the bottle of wine in the fridge.

Now plan your own murder mystery. Include three details – a newspaper, a one-way ticket and a lipstick. Use them any way you wish. For instance, the newspaper could be important for its contents, like the advertisement for the Red-Headed League, or as proof of a date or as incriminating evidence. Do what you like with them, so long as you find some way of bringing them into a plot. No need to fill in a complete plot. You are learning how to fit the pieces together like a jigsaw. Some gaps can be left for later.

Activity 6   Finding your detective

In these exercises, we have concentrated mostly on structure and narrative drive. But of course there are other components in a good yarn. One element is bold characterization, another a strong sense of place. These two are united in the fictional detective. Rankin's Inspector Rebus is rooted in Edinburgh. Sherlock Holmes is unimaginable without those foggy London streets. Crime fiction contains a great deal of social observation. The detective studies the patterns of human behaviour, watching for any deviation from the norm.

Invent your own detective, a policeman like Rebus, an amateur like Holmes or a private investigator like Dashiell Hammett's Sam Spade. Rankin and Conan Doyle locate their detectives in their own neighbourhood, on streets they've walked themselves. But H. R. F. Keating invented Inspector Ghote without ever having set foot in Bombay, and other crime writers have set their stories in the distant past. Whatever the territory, immerse yourself in your fictional universe, a world your detective knows inside out.

Once you've found the right environment for your detective, write a character profile. If, like Holmes, they have a sidekick, describe them through the eyes of that other person. Don't be too nervous about authenticity if you're writing a police procedural. Obviously there has to be some credibility, but fictional inspectors like Wexford bear little resemblance to their real-life counterparts.

Activity 7   Research

'O Death, Where is Thy Spatula?' showed the value of research in writing yarns. If you are an expert on any subject, exploit that information. If you know an expert, pick their brains. Married to a chef, Brite deploys a professional's knowledge of the restaurant scene. Every job, however undemanding, generates its own rituals and demands specialist knowledge that you may take for granted. In crime fiction, factual details are indispensable. Talk to your friends about their jobs and their hobbies. The most harmless activity can provide the means to murder. In Lionel Davidson's 'Indian Rope Trick' (Edwards 2003), a technique for salmon-fishing covers up the perfect crime.

As well as using first-hand experience, try researching something new. The German author W. G. Sebald recommended research as a cure for writer's block: 'Every writer knows that sometimes the best ideas come to you when you are reading something else, say, something about Bismarck, and then suddenly between the lines your head starts drifting, and you arrive at the ideas you need' (Mühling 2003: 18). Sebald's 'disorderly research' (2003) is more a way of releasing the unconscious than planting deliberate clues. But obscure details like the deadly mushrooms in 'Means of Evil' are very handy in crime fiction. If you're very clever, you can even make up your own poisonous plants or chemical compounds. Surf the Net. Look up encyclopaedia at random. Sherlock Holmes's familiarity with tattoo marks doesn't help him solve the mystery of the Red-Headed League. But he proves his powers of observation by analysing the little fish near Wilson's wrist.

Read the papers for insights into motive and the investigative process. Criminals often give themselves away unconsciously. For instance, in a British murder trial, the accused was reported as having spoken of the victims in the past tense at a time when no one knew for certain they were dead. Be a magpie. Steal facts to build your fiction. As Holmes himself says, 'For strange effects and extraordinary combinations we must go to life itself, which is far more daring than any effort of the imagination' (Conan Doyle 1994: 30).

Activity 8   The Locked Room

The impossible crime is a venerable tradition, dating back to Poe's 'The Murders in the Rue Morgue'. A body is discovered in some place where a murderer could have not have gained access – such as a room locked on the inside. In H. R. F. Keating's 'The Hound of the Hanging Gardens' (Edwards 2003), the victim is found in a park where the gates are locked at night. Devise your own locked-room mystery. It need not be inside a house, or even necessarily a room.

Activity 9   The Warped Mind

Short fiction is especially suited to intense psychological studies. Writers like Patricia Highsmith and Margaret Yorke take us inside the criminal mind, exploring the boundaries of 'normal' behaviour, sometimes with comic effect and sometimes, at a deeper level, grappling with the nature of evil. In Julian Symons's chilling 'The Tigers of Subtopia' (Edwards 2003), a group of middle-aged commuters turn vigilante against the young working-class 'louts' beyond their private estate. In Margaret Yorke's 'The Liberator', a retired schoolmistress quietly disposes of fellow tourists she finds especially annoying. The trick is to push commonplace emotions to an extreme, so that characters act upon their impulses. Is there a type of person you could cheerfully push off a cliff? Imagine the kind of person who'd carry it through, and describe how it's done from their point of view. Acting the psychopath may make you feel just a little uneasy. But remember, after all, it *is* just a story.

2

Capturing the moment

Some stories are based on imagery rather than plot. The British writer Ali Smith compares the short story to a stone thrown in a pond. 'If you throw a stone in the water, you see concentric circles. You know that something has been changed or moved and in a moment it's going to be gone' (Gapper 2003: 14). The photographer Henri Cartier-Bresson famously spoke about the 'decisive moment'. Like the photographer, the short-story writer can recognize that instant which encapsulates an experience, and give it expression. Like photographs, short stories can bring emotions alive through the power of the image.

One of my own stories, 'Twentieth Frame' (Blackburn et al. 1984: 116), is conceived as a series of snapshots. Geoffrey, the first-person narrator, serves as a camera; we see each numbered 'frame' through his mind's eye:

1. Light knifes through the open window. My head aches from the train journey, and now from George's talk, driving too fast round the lanes. '. . . In a few years it'll pay for itself . . .' Her arm stretched towards the farthest corner of the glass, she leans out, Windowlene in hand. Scarf on head. Without hair, a face as innocent as a baby doll. I screw my eyes to catch the round eyes and the mouth in the sun. When she sees us coming, she

waves. She smiles, but she keeps herself vacant. You must be Joyce.

(Blackburn et al. 1984: 116)

The story is assembled as a kind of montage, built from Geoffrey's thoughts and impressions. When I started writing the story I wasn't sure where it was going, but, by exploring ideas about photography, voyeurism and the visual, I found a plot emerging of its own accord. Imagery creates unity in a fragmented narrative. Image-based fiction tends to give characters more psychological complexity than is possible in the traditional 'yarn'. When Cartier-Bresson made his observations on photography, he commented on the perfect fusion of form and content in the photographic image. The same applies to prose. If you get the language and imagery right, meaning will be generated by the techniques you have – consciously or unconsciously – chosen to apply.

If you are writing a novel, the narrative usually unfolds over long stretches of time. Characters age and evolve; themes and patterns gradually develop. One of the biggest pitfalls facing new writers is trying to cram too much inside one story. You do not have the space for the sort of timescale you expect from reading novels. This is why you are often told to stick to a single incident or just one character. In fact, it is possible to break this rule. Alice Munro, whose work I discuss in Chapter 6, manages to condense whole lifetimes into a single story; while Jorge Luis Borges (see Chapter 4) can fit an entire universe. Nonetheless, most short-stories are set within a limited time frame. If you have read any contemporary novelists who also produce short stories – for instance, Margaret Atwood, John Updike or Ian McEwan – you might find it useful to compare their work across genres. Where a novel might trace a character's situation back to childhood or even span the generations, a story is more likely to crystallize their experiences within a particular crisis point, played out across days or hours rather than months or years.

In the early part of the twentieth century, writers like James Joyce, Katherine Mansfield, Virginia Woolf and William Faulkner were especially interested in the short story's ability to capture the passing moment. Influenced by Freudian concepts of the unconscious and by the philosopher Bergson's ideas about the flow of time, these writers wanted to engage with a fleeting and ever-changing reality. So far as they were concerned, the tidy plots and neat endings of conventional fiction distorted real-life experience. These 'modernist' experiments in short fiction also had an impact on the novel. One obvious exception to my generalizations about time in the novel is Joyce's *Ulysses* where events take place in a single day. However the chapters of *Ulysses* are self-contained episodes told in different styles, rather like interlinked stories. Short fiction still offers endless opportunities to experiment, especially through hypertext (some sites are listed at the end of the book). Later in the chapter we'll look at 'non-linear' narrative which reorders chronological time.

Critics have perceived a split between stories influenced by modernism and the old-fashioned yarn, between plot-driven and image-based fiction. For the purposes of this chapter, I am keeping to that distinction, while still being aware that there are many stories crossing the divide. Psychological thrillers often introduce a high level of ambiguity into a plot-driven narrative. I classified Henry James's 'The Turn of the Screw' as a yarn in the previous chapter, but I could also have referred to it in this chapter because it represents the world through a character's distorted consciousness. As I explained in my introduction, the genres overlap. You can benefit from both traditions, whatever your personal preference; and when it comes to your own writing you may ultimately find such distinctions irrelevant.

In the previous chapter, I used the concept of the yarn to show how storytellers have built suspense and created narrative drive, using tricks that date back to the oral tradition. These elements are less important in image-based fiction, which is developed from thoughts and impressions. In this chapter, I'm going to examine stories by Mansfield and Joyce to show how imagery can be used to take you inside a character's mind, exploring memories and perceptions. I will show you how to structure a story around the 'epiphany' and discuss the merits of the 'open ending'. Then we'll move on to James Kelman, a contemporary Scottish writer, in a further discussion of the 'stream of consciousness' technique. All of these examples show the benefits of setting a story within a restricted time frame.

Using the senses: 'Bliss' (Katherine Mansfield, 1920)

Katherine Mansfield's 'Bliss' plunges straight into the changing moods and impressions of her heroine, Bertha, as she lives through a single day:

> Although Bertha Young was thirty she still had moments like this
> when she wanted to run instead of walk, to take dancing steps on

and off the pavement, to bowl a hoop, to throw something up in
the air and catch it again, or to stand still and laugh at – nothing –
at nothing, simply.

What can you do if you are thirty and, turning the corner of
your own street, you are overcome, suddenly, by a feeling of bliss –
absolute bliss! as though you'd suddenly swallowed a bright piece
of the late afternoon sun and it burned in your bosom, sending out
a little shower of sparks into every particle, into every finger and
toe? . . .

(Mansfield 1984: 91–2)

Mansfield records Bertha's feelings. She also reproduces them in long,
breathless, repetitious sentences. The broken syntax of 'a feeling of bliss –
absolute bliss!', full of dashes and explanation marks, make the language
seem spontaneous, like someone thinking out loud. This writer is not just
telling us *about* Bertha. She is taking us inside Bertha's skin, sharing her
insights moment by moment.

But what is it really like to be you or me or any other individual? How
do you describe the myriad sensations, complex trains of thoughts and
contradictory emotions that make up one person's consciousness? You
can't. But you can suggest them through imagery. Mansfield uses vivid
sensual details to make you imagine physically all of those things you
can't put into words. A feeling 'as though you'd suddenly swallowed a
bright piece of the late afternoon sun and it burned in your bosom, sending out a little shower of sparks into every particle, into every finger and
toe' can't really be defined. But it can be evoked as a physical sensation.

Mansfield returns to images of heat and cold throughout 'Bliss', referring back to 'that bright glowing place – that shower of little sparks
coming from it' (Mansfield 1984: 92). As the story progresses, the metaphor of sun and sparks becomes a form of shorthand for Bertha's state of
mind. 'Imagery' is not restricted to the visual. Image-based writing
exploits all the senses, including touch, taste and smell.

'Bliss' does have a plot and a tight dramatic structure. We follow
Bertha as she prepares to hold a dinner party, sharing her anticipation
and her disillusionment when things don't quite go to plan. But, unlike
the yarns we looked at in the first chapter, the narrative is not 'plot-
driven'. It is fuelled by what's happening inside the characters rather than
external actions. Often it is unclear exactly what is going on in the world
around them.

Bertha is very taken with one of her dinner guests, Miss Fulton. She imagines that there will be some sort of rapport established between them, and there does seem to be a moment of wordless communion as the two women stand at a window gazing out at a pear tree in blossom. Once again, Mansfield uses images of fire and light and gives the scene emotional resonance through vivid description: 'Although it was so still it seemed, like the flame of a candle, to stretch up, to point, to quiver in the bright air, to grow taller and taller as they gazed – almost to touch the rim of the round, silver moon' (Mansfield 1984: 102).

The description is full of movement. This sense of restlessness runs through the narrative, suggesting quickly changing moods and shifting impressions, the dynamism of life. And indeed the mood changes a few pages later, when Bertha glimpses her husband up to something in the hallway:

> And she saw . . . Harry with Miss Fulton's coat in his arms and Miss Fulton with her back turned to him and her head bent. He tossed the coat away, put his hands on her shoulders and turned her violently to him. His lips said: 'I adore you,' and Miss Fulton laid her moonbeam fingers on his cheeks and smiled her sleepy smile. Harry's nostrils quivered; his lips curled back in a hideous grin while he whispered: 'To-morrow,' and with her eyelids Miss Fulton said: 'Yes'.
>
> (Mansfield 1984: 105)

All of this is seen in a moment, in the turn of a head, and while some details are stark, others are very ambiguous. We are reading Bertha's interpretation of something she has witnessed, or seems to have witnessed. While a plot-driven story offers us the satisfaction of narrative closure – a definite ending – nothing is finally resolved here. We don't know if Harry is really having an affair with Miss Fulton, whether Bertha confronts him, or whether she ignores what she has seen.

The pear tree is the story's central image, appearing at its emotional climax and sounding its final note in the closing sentence:

> 'Oh, what is going to happen now?' she cried. But the pear tree was as lovely as ever and as full of flower and as still.
>
> (Mansfield 1984: 105)

Mansfield harnesses the vibrancy of the natural world to convey intense emotions. Here, the pear tree suggests something that is alive and growing, yet is also timeless. Miss Fulton's 'moonbeam fingers' repeats the image of the moon behind the tree. Her green and white outfit echoes its colours. Imagery enables us to read patterns of meaning, but what those meanings are remains open to question. Like many image-based stories, 'Bliss' has an 'open ending'. That closing sentence might suggest all kinds of things – that nature carries on regardless, or that Bertha is consoled by the pear tree. We just don't know and, like Bertha herself, we can only guess what happens next.

The yarns we discussed in the previous chapter all move towards plot resolution. In 'The Fall of the House of Usher', Poe stages a grand finale, as Madeline rises from the grave and the mansion splits in two. In 'The Red-Headed League', the villain is unmasked. An open ending leaves something for the reader to ponder. It often operates like a freeze-frame, suddenly leaving the character poised in mid-air, on the verge of a crucial decision.

A recent example of an open ending is in Nell Freudenberger's 'The Orphan'. This story is told from the viewpoint of Alice, an American, whose daughter Mandy is working in Bangkok. The whole family is paying a Christmas visit, but the trip is fraught with problems. Alice and her husband Jeff are planning to announce to both their children that they have separated; and Alice is deeply disturbed when Mandy introduces a man she previously claimed had raped and beaten her as her steady boyfriend. As if that weren't enough, Alice's son is also giving her grief with his self-righteous politics. At the end of the story, the announcement has been made, resulting in the younger generation walking out in a sulk. Left in their twin room, the couple make love:

> They know what each other likes, and they've never been so considerate; it's almost choreographed. When it's finished, he prepares to hold her and she thoughtfully absolves him of this responsibility. He expresses his gratitude by staying in this bed, and she moves as far from him as possible, although it's not necessary. There's already enough sheet between them, and the mattress is firm enough that you wouldn't know there was another person in the bed except for the irregular, wakeful breathing. She lies absolutely still anyway, and after a while it begins to feel as if there

is something there, something delicate in the space between them, which they must be careful not to roll over and crush.

(Freudenberger 2003: 65–6)

Although the event seems natural and inevitable, it is also shocking behaviour in people who are supposed to be getting divorced. Alice's movements suggest that it's a temporary aberration, but we can only guess what the future might actually hold. Open endings invite us to speculate, and not all readers will reach the same conclusion. The story's title, 'The Orphan', brings us back to an earlier epiphany when Alice and her husband visit the orphanage where Mandy works. Jeff is quite taken by one particular baby, and Alice finds herself contemplating adoption, imagining 'too much food in the refrigerator, piles of things on the stairs that no one ever takes up, broken crayons at the bottom of her purse' (Freudenberger 2003: 58). Her thoughts are never communicated verbally to Jeff, but here, as in the final paragraph, Freudenberger suggests a kind of telepathy between a couple who've been together all these years. In that closing passage, the 'something delicate in the space between them' refers to all kinds of intangible feelings, but it also makes us picture a baby lying there. Freudenberger doesn't tell us whether they go back to pick up the child who, in any case, has a very small part to play in the events of the story, but that is a possible interpretation. Although we do not return to an explicit image at the end, the orphan provides a central image which unifies and closes the story, just like Bertha's pear tree.

Open endings add subtlety to your writing, reminding us how unfathomable the human heart can be. But you can't just stop because you've run out of ideas. The ending should be carefully paced. The reader senses that the narrative is winding down. In 'Bliss', the moments between Bertha's discovery and her final contemplation of the pear tree are filled with trivial bits of dialogue as her guests leave the party. In 'The Orphan', we are prepared for the closing passage by a description of the first time Alice and Jeff made love, way back in 1967. In general, it is wise to jump straight into a story at the start, as Mansfield does with 'Bliss', and to linger over the ending. Returning to a central image will help you find your way.

As we have seen in this section, images are inherently ambiguous. They do not form a code for the reader to simply decipher. Image-based stories uncover mysteries which can never be fully explained. Raymond Carver summons this sense of mystery when he quotes V. S. Pritchett's definition of the short story as 'something glimpsed from the corner of the eye, in passing' (Carver 1998: xiii). We might think of Bertha here, glimpsing something strange going on in the hallway. Carver then goes on to describe 'the glimpse given life turned into something that will illuminate the moment and just maybe lock it indelibly into the reader's consciousness' (Carver 1998: xiii).

In the exercises at the end of the chapter, we'll explore ways of capturing passing moments, using the senses to generate images from the unconscious. We have touched on this already in Chapter 1 when I encouraged you to tap into your nightmares and phobias. Imagery plays an essential part in most types of fiction, and you may well find that for you, as for many other writers, most stories start from a compelling image – whether it's something from your own imagination or something you've witnessed in real life. Keeping a notebook will help you record these images. I will have plenty to say about notebooks when we reach the activities. In the meantime, I want to think about structuring imagery using one of the most common short-story techniques, the epiphany.

Epiphany: 'The Dead' (James Joyce, 1914)

Like 'Bliss', 'The Dead' focuses on a party, using a single event to bring a character's life to a moment of crisis. This time it's the annual dance held by two elderly music teachers in Dublin. As the familiar ritual unfolds, their nephew, Gabriel, becomes increasingly aware of their fragility and the transience of life. As they make their way back to the hotel, his attention turns to his wife, Gretta. Like Bertha, Gabriel is prone to sudden whims, though his mood is described rather more explicitly:

> She leaned lightly on his arm, as lightly as when she had danced with him a few hours before. He had felt proud and happy then, happy that she was his, proud of her grace and wifely carriage. But now, after the kindling again of so many memories, the first touch of her body, musical and strange and perfumed, sent through him a keen pang of lust.

> (Joyce 1961: 212)

Joyce is trying to put into words feelings that can barely be expressed, things you can't quite put your finger on. They are turned into physical sensations, responses to the world around him. 'Musical and strange and perfumed' describes not Gretta's body exactly, but 'the first touch of her body', and that word 'musical' suggests movement and change. In itself, music has no meaning; it is pure sensation. By referring to music so often in his story Joyce emphasizes everything that is instinctive and intuitive in our everyday lives.

Gabriel's passion is thwarted. Gretta is in an odd frame of mind, pensive and detached. It turns out that a song has reminded her of an old love affair from her girlhood and the premature death of her sweetheart, Michael Furey. She becomes distraught over a whole stretch of her life that Gabriel knew nothing about, reliving the moment when, leaving his sickbed, her lover turns up outside her bedroom window:

> 'I implored of him to go back home at once and told him he would get his death in the rain. But he said he did not want to live. I can see his eyes as well as well! He was standing at the end of the wall where there was a tree.'

> (Joyce 1961: 218)

Gretta leaves her home in the west of Ireland to go to school in Dublin; one week later, news follows that Michael has died. Her revelation shows us how little we can know about even those who seem closest to us: 'He thought of how she who lay beside him had locked in her heart for so many years that image of her lover's eyes when he told her that he did not wish to live' (Joyce 1961: 219). Arthur Schnitzler's novella *Dream Story* (later filmed by Stanley Kubrick as *Eyes Wide Shut*) plays with a similar idea. A happily married man discovers that his wife has a secret erotic life, in her fantasies and in her dreams. The person sleeping next to you may actually be somewhere else.

Gabriel imagines the scenes described by Gretta, picturing in the darkness the hazy outline of Michael Furey standing under the tree:

> Other forms were near. His soul had approached that region where dwell the vast hosts of the dead. He was conscious of, but could not apprehend, their wayward and flickering existence. His own

identity was fading out into a grey impalpable world: the solid world itself, which these dead had one time reared and lived in, was dissolving and dwindling.

(Joyce 1961: 220)

Nothing is resolved between Gabriel and Gretta. Like 'Bliss', 'The Dead' has an open ending. The closing image is of snow covering Ireland, from Dublin to the west coast, where Gretta's sweetheart lies buried. The final sentence is hypnotic, almost an incantation: 'His soul swooned slowly as he heard the snow falling faintly through the universe and faintly falling, like the descent of their last end, upon all the living and the dead' (Joyce 1961: 220).

Joyce coined the term 'epiphany' to describe a moment of intense insight, which briefly illuminates the whole of existence. In image-based fiction, it serves as an emotional turning point, replacing the moment of outward revelation or decisive action which performs this function in a story dependent on plot. In a plot-driven story, a revelation leads towards a final resolution grounded in external action. An epiphany in image-based fiction hints at subjective, personal meanings hidden beneath the surface, which may or may not lead to action. In 'The Dead', Gretta's outburst triggers this process. In another of Joyce's *Dubliners* stories, 'Eveline', it is the sound of a street organ as Eveline prepares to elope. The tune revives, in Eveline's mind, the moment when she promised her dying mother she would keep the home together. This epiphany does bring about an external change, reversing her decision. But the effect is implied; it is not made explicit. 'Bliss' contains an apparently perfect epiphany when Bertha and Miss Fulton gaze upon the pear tree. But the magic is rapidly deflated by the business with Bertha's husband. Such moments are sometimes described as 'false' epiphany; the fictional character awaits transformation, only to be disappointed, or else to fool herself.

Epiphanies are usually invisible and private. On the outside, things seem pretty much as usual. It's very important that they take place inside the everyday, subtly altering the character's perceptions and making time seem to stand still. The mystical vision of the snow in 'The Dead' is triggered partly by an ordinary phrase from the weather report: 'snow was general all over Ireland' (Joyce 1961: 220). They are also spontaneous, beyond our control and, as these examples have shown, linked to submerged memories.

Many of you will share the experience of suddenly hearing a song that that brings back memories. Radio stations often play requests with some anecdote attached from the listener. Many other stimuli, pleasant or unpleasant, can bring back memories; a friend of mine can't eat custard because it reminds him of his schooldays. In stories like 'The Dead', Joyce captures the way these associations rise to the surface of everyday life.

The clock ticks in a linear fashion; despite the promises made by cosmetic manufacturers, you cannot turn back time. Yet one's consciousness does drift backwards and forwards; subjectively, time is not strictly linear. This fluid experience of time is explored by Joyce and Mansfield, through the epiphany and the image. Using a shifting time frame can be exciting for the writer and a challenge for the reader. In the next section, I look at more recent image-based fiction and at non-linear structure.

Playing around with time

Many short stories still turn on the epiphany. In the Irish writer William Trevor's 'After Rain', Harriet is at a loose end. Now her boyfriend has finished with her, their holiday is cancelled, so in desperation she books in at an Italian resort she remembers from childhood. Valiantly, she goes through the motions. She reads. She looks at a painting in a church. Stepping out of the church, something strikes her:

> While she stands alone among the dripping vines she cannot make a connection that she knows is there. There is a blankness in her thoughts, a density that feels like a muddle also, until she realizes: the Annunciation was painted after rain. Its distant landscape, glimpsed through arches, has the temporary look that she is seeing now. It was after rain that the angel came: those first cool moments were a chosen time.
>
> (Trevor 1996: 94)

When Harriet reaches her understanding, time seems to stand still, just as it did for Bertha and for Gabriel. The American Matthew Klam's 'There Should Be a Name for It' gives us a painstaking account of a young woman clumsily roasting a chicken:

> She grabs it by the cavity, sticks it on its back in the pan, and

throws in a bunch of herb leaves and pine nuts. Then she cuts up an onion and an orange with the skin still on.

My office mate Amy told me, after she had her baby, how similar an uncooked chicken felt in her hands to the body of her daughter. She said how she held it, rubbing olive oil on it, under the wings, around the thighs, with soft loose pink skin, the small protective rib cage.

(Cassini and Testa 2003: 19)

Klam exploits the erotic overtones of the imagery and the very word 'baby', as his narrator's thoughts turn from cooking to sex: 'I want to bare her breast and nod on her nipple. I'm her baby. She's my baby. Everybody's somebody's baby. Lets make a baby' (Cassini and Testa 2003: 20).

Gradually the time shifts to a few months earlier, describing the narrator's girlfriend Lynn's pregnancy and abortion. When the narrative returns to the present, it becomes clear that the tensions between the narrator and Lynn, and the narrator's intense admiration for her, are about something more than cooking dinner. Although we know about the abortion already, the epiphany shows us its true impact, making us reassess the earlier parts of the story.

In their millennial anthology, *All Hail the New Puritans*, two British writers, Nicholas Blincoe and Matt Thorne turned their back on the modernist legacy, rejecting shifting time frames and, by implication, the epiphany. In an attempt, as they saw it, to bring literature up to date, they issued a 'New Puritan Manifesto', inspired by the Dogme manifesto drawn by Lars von Trier and other Scandinavian filmmakers. Like the Dogme manifesto, it was a tongue-in-cheek exercise, imposing rules on their contributors in a stern tone of voice. Rule 5 declared that: 'In the name of clarity, we recognize the importance of temporal linearity and eschew flashbacks, dual temporal narratives and foreshadowing' (Blincoe and Thorne 2001). They wanted fiction to be more like film, which they saw as the leading narrative medium. Yet at the beginning of the twenty-first century, film itself has played around with time in cult classics such as *Memento*, *Donnie Darko*, *Amores Perros* and *21 Grammes*. If you have seen any of these films, consider how they move backwards and forwards through time. Each one of them is structured in a different way; could that structure work in a short story?

Like *Memento*, a recent story by a new British writer, Ann Clarkson, reverses the order of events, splitting the narrative into short sections, each headed by space–time coordinates. 'Morning Chemistry' begins '**0900hrs** *Outside the chemistry lab*' and ends '**0830hrs** *The store cupboard*'. In cool, detached language, the story runs backwards through half an hour in an ordinary school:

> **0900hrs** *Outside the chemistry lab*
> His year-11 form straighten up against the wall when they hear the door swing, his heels approaching military-style in the science corridor. He walks *allegro* towards the line of fractious, chattering pupils. His eyes sweep along, taking in missing ties, short skirts, eyeliner, nail-varnish, body piercing.
>
> (Clarkson 2003: 33)

Gradually, the teacher's inner life is revealed, as we slowly rewind towards 8.30 a.m. in the store cupboard, where he had sex with the music teacher, Madeline. The clue's already there in Clarkson's musical notations, his movements becoming '*largo*' or '*pianissimo*' according to the situation. Mundane reality clashes with fevered eroticism; and of course the title itself puns on this tension. Unlike the stories by Mansfield, Joyce, Trevor, Klam and Freudenberger, 'Morning Chemistry' does not contain an epiphany. But all the stories consist of a patchwork of images, moods and impressions. In all of them, we are encouraged to find a meaning by reading between the lines. In 'Morning Chemistry', the full significance of the musical imagery only becomes clear when we discover that Madeline likes playing Mozart when she's having sex. We piece the story together, reading backwards, forwards and across, filling in the gaps.

This may seem daunting to those of you just starting to write fiction. How could you construct something so complicated, with so many layers of meaning? To find one answer, think back to my description of my own story 'Twentieth Frame'. Think of writing your story as assembling a montage. You don't have to start at the beginning or have an overall plan. If you concentrate on the language and the imagery, the connections will form gradually of their own accord.

Stream of consciousness: 'Not Not While the Giro'
(James Kelman, 1983)

Image-based stories give you the opportunity to really improvise, revelling in language for its own sake. James Kelman's 'Not Not While the Giro' is virtuoso prose, drawing on Glaswegian speech and defying the laws of punctuation. We saw earlier how 'Bliss' plunges in and out of Bertha's consciousness and delivers an open ending. 'Not Not While the Giro' opens even more abruptly, suggesting that we are catching up with an ongoing story:

> of tea so I can really enjoy this 2nd last smoke which will be very very strong which is of course why I drink tea with it in a sense to counteract the harm it must do my inners. Not that tea cures cancer poisoning or even guards against nicotine – helps unclog my mouth a little. Maybe it doesnt. My mouth tastes bad. Hot and kind of squelchy. I am smoking too much old tobacco.
>
> (Kelman 1995: 182)

This is a stylized version of thinking out loud, often called 'interior monologue', and in fact it's quite easy to imagine this type of passage performed on stage or radio. Kelman claims that he is an outlet for voices suppressed by mainstream British literature which is dominated by the English middle classes. This passage resonates with the rhythms and phraseology of the story – 'in a sense to counteract the harm', 'cancer poisoning', 'hot and kind of squelchy'.

An interior monologue can be integrated into a third-person narrative. If you look again at the opening passage of 'Bliss' and the closing sections of 'The Dead' you will see how this is done. The protagonist's thoughts are woven into authorial description, using their own language. The term 'stream of consciousness' refers more specifically to a first-person narrative mimicking the jumble of thoughts, emotions and memories passing through our minds at any moment – many of them incoherent or mundane. Consciousness has no beginning – at least, not one we can remember. No wonder the narrative starts in midstream. It cuts out just as suddenly when we reach the end. The narrator's responses are registered in a direct commentary – 'hot and kind of squelchy'. In 'stream of consciousness' nothing is explained, though much may be revealed indirectly through reflections sparked off by sense impressions.

A committed socialist, angered by social inequality, Kelman wants to show us harsh reality as it is experienced by those, like his narrator, who subsist on welfare benefits. The day consists of the small rituals he has constructed around his diminishing supply of tea and tobacco, while he thinks up schemes to get through the two days till his cheque arrives. With nothing to do, every trivial action takes on significance:

> It isnt as bad as all that; here I am and it is now the short a.m.'s. The short a.m.'s. I await the water boiling for a final cup of tea. Probably only drink the stuff in order to pish. Does offer a sort of relief. And simply strolling to the kitchenette and preparing this tea: the gushing tap, the kettle, gathering the tea-bag from the crumb strewn shelf – all of this is motion.
>
> (Kelman 1995: 194)

The irregular punctuation, removing the apostrophes from 'isn't' and 'doesn't', keep the flow of thought intact, while the repeated phrases suggests someone stuck in a rut. Yet, although the narrator seems to be rambling, the language is controlled and carefully pared down. Kelman writes in short, jagged sentences, interspersed with longer digressions like the final sentence in the paragraph above. Using natural speech patterns and selective repetition, he builds up a poetic rhythm. This is how he solves the problem of describing tedium without boring the reader. The highly charged style compensates the reader for the dreariness of the content. When the narrator speculates about his elderly neighbour, the language is charged by his romantic fantasies:

> A man probably wronged her many years ago. Jilted. With her beautiful 16 year old younger sister by her as bridesmaid, an engagement ring on her finger just decorously biding her time till this marriage of her big sister is out the way so she can step in and get married to her own youthful admirer, and on the other side of poor old Mrs Soinson stood her widowed father or should I say sat since he would have been an invalid and in his carriage, only waiting his eldest daughter's marriage so he can join his dearly departed who died in childbirth (that of the beautiful 16 year old) up there in heaven.
>
> (Kelman 1995: 195)

Kelman's protagonist has several grand plans, which show little sign of fruition. He might for instance walk from Land's End to John O'Groats if only he could make up his mind. At the end of the story, you know nothing is likely to change. Fundamentally, this is a story about killing time and inertia. Out of a description of the most humdrum experiences comes something universal about the human condition.

I am not saying that Kelman necessarily set out to prove impressive existential truths – rather that such truths might arise unbidden from raw material that may seem slight or unpromising. You can write about anything and make it interesting. You don't have to cast about for an exciting plot or even to have any idea where your story's going until quite late in the drafting process.

Janice Galloway, a Scottish contemporary of James Kelman, also uses internal monologues and stream of consciousness effectively. Some of her very short stories are based on extended first-person descriptions. Starting with the simple statement 'Nobody kisses like Derek', 'Where You Find It' develops into a dizzying analysis of the character's snogging technique. Only towards the end, when the narrator lets slip that 'I wouldn't let any other bastard do it, not even if they ask, not even if they're good looking or offer extra', do we realize the full significance of that opening line (Galloway 1996: 17–18). These very compressed stories build up a poetic rhythm grounded in natural speech patterns. Look, for instance, at the stark opening of 'Bisex':

I worry.
Sometimes I need to hear your voice.

I worry. I phone.
You are often out when I phone.
(Galloway 1996: 87)

In the activities that follow, I begin with strategies for writing unself-consciously, responding to visual stimuli and harnessing all of the senses. When attempting the exercises, don't worry too much about getting them 'right'. It is more important to write spontaneously without preconceptions than to follow my instructions to the letter. The material you generate can then be incorporated into fictional pieces, using the epiphany, open endings, non-linear structures and stream of consciousness. Some of the exercises are based on personal and autobiographical approaches which you will use again in Chapter 6. When we reach that chapter, there will be some discussion of the relationship between autobiographical material and fiction. In the meantime, plunder your memories. They are much too good to waste.

Activity 1   Journals, notebooks, bus tickets and scrap paper

Most creative-writing handbooks advise you to keep some kind of journal. Some of the material may find its way into your fiction, but its main function is to help you get into the habit of writing. If you use a camera, you'll know that if you carry it regularly you'll find things to photograph. Most of those pictures will be fairly ordinary, but one of them will be as close to perfect as you'll ever get. A camera or a notebook frames the world in a different way. It makes you more alert to the images and words around you.

In her letters, Katherine Mansfield often spoke about the joys of solitary observation:

> It is such a strange delight to observe people and to try to understand them, to walk over the mountains and into the valleys of the world, and fields and road and to move on rivers and seas, to arrive late at night in strange cities or to come into little harbours just at pink dawn when its cold with a high wind blowing somewhere *up* in the air, to push through the heavy door into little cafés and to watch the pattern people make among tables & bottles and glasses, to watch women when they are off their guard, and to get them to talk then, to smell flowers and leaves and fruit and grass – all this – and all this is nothing – for there is so much more.
>
> (Mansfield 1989: 54)

This passage is bursting with energy. It is quite raw, even clumsy, with at least one punctuation error. If she was writing for publication, she might have adjusted the odd phrase – for instance, 'get them to talk then'. But the extract's vitality derives from its spontaneity. This is the sort of excitement you need to find in writing for its own sake. Notebook-writing doesn't have to prove anything or be shown to anyone. Mine's indecipherable anyway.

Most creative-writing handbooks insist that you should write every day. My concern here is that keeping the notebook may become a chore like brushing your teeth before you go to bed. If you can manage it, fine, but don't just go through the motions. The idea is to liberate your creativity, not to restrict your own freedom. Write whenever you find an opportunity. I have to confess that I've sometimes started scribbling during an especially mind-numbing meeting. I've described the people, the room – anything – while the bureaucrats assumed I was eagerly making notes. Writing is your escape hatch.

At some point you will have to buckle down. Completing a short story requires a certain amount of self-discipline. In the later stages, the editing process is, quite honestly, boring – as the inventor Edison famously said, genius is ninety per cent perspiration. But writing doesn't just mean sitting still at a desk. Ideas, phrases and images often jolt into action when you're on the move, which is why so many of my best stories have started on the back of a bus ticket. You won't always remember to keep your notebook with you, but never go anywhere without a pen. Remember what Mansfield said about arriving late at night in strange cities or pushing through the heavy door into little cafés. Natalie Goldberg's *Writing Down the Bones* has further suggestions on notebook writing.

Activity 2 I am a camera

Discussing my own story, 'Twentieth Frame', I described the narrator as a sort of camera. When you are writing observationally in your notebook, think of yourself as the camera's eye, taking snapshots with words instead of film. You can also make use of an actual camera. In his collection of character studies, *The Emigrants*, the German fiction writer W. G. Sebald follows his usual habit by including various black-and-white snapshots and postcards. These are often small and grainy, not glossy or well presented. But their presence adds to the complex network of observations and memories in the book.

Get hold of a basic camera – nothing fancy. A disposable one will do. There are several ways in which you can use photography to enhance your skill in capturing the moment.

Find a crowd, perhaps at a football match or an outdoor concert. City streets are especially good for this because so many different kinds of people are jostling side by side. You need to be sensitive because some people object to being photographed. If you decide to take a picture of an individual it is polite to ask their permission, even if this means they start self-consciously posing. For the most part, you are shooting fairly randomly, using up at least one roll of film. Don't worry about composition. Your pictures are not intended to be technically proficient. When the pictures are developed, choose a face in the crowd. Describe the thoughts going through their head at the moment when you took the photograph.

Choose three different locations, this time somewhere without any crowds – for example, the city first thing on Sunday morning, a country hillside, a quiet café. They need not be absolutely deserted, but the atmosphere should be at least a little lonely. You could even use a place from the previous exercise when the crowds are gone. When you have a selection of photographs, imagine them as stills from a movie. Tell the story of that imaginary film.

Use close-up. The great Russian writer Chekhov said that by describing a part of something you could capture the whole:

> In nature descriptions one should seize upon small details, grouping them in such a way that you can see the whole picture when you close your eyes. For example, you'll capture a moonlit night if you tell how a shiver of glass from a broken bottle gleamed like a bright star in the weir, and the black shadow of a dog or wolf rolled past . . .
>
> (Chekhov 1994: 32)

Following Chekhov's advice, take some close-ups in a place you know well. Really look at the small details you may not have noticed – a broken bottle in your gutter, a poster on someone's wall. Write a short descriptive piece (about 500 words) based on the two images which you feel were most effective in conveying mood and atmosphere.

Activity 3   A picture paints a thousand words

Continuing the work on visual imagery, visit an art gallery, preferably somewhere not too busy. Take your time, wander round and choose a picture – any kind of picture, painting, drawing, print or photograph. It can be an abstract if you like, because the object is more to absorb the mood of the picture than to describe what it represents. Sit down and contemplate that picture. Really look. Take in colours and shape and texture. And don't forget its setting in the gallery itself. Galleries can be friendly and welcoming, but they can also be quite eerie. You may pick up on footsteps, whispers, the traffic outside or a distant clatter from the café.

If there is a café that might be a good place to sit while you write for twenty minutes. You are writing as freely as possible, starting with the idea that the picture you've seen will be an illustration for the finished story or descriptive piece. As I have said, you don't necessarily have to work out a story the picture is telling. You are trying to achieve in words what the picture conveys in purely visual terms.

Activity 4   Before and after

This exercise continues working with visual images as a means of 'capturing the moment'. British writer Alex Garland's 'Monaco' follows the minutes before a photograph is taken. The photographer is in a rather dangerous position at a racetrack. He starts snapping a pretty girl in the restaurant overlooking the track. Responding to the camera, she becomes – to put it mildly – increasingly intimate with her companion. The story itself becomes a kind of race against time as the photographer anticipates the perfect shot. The story's final paragraph *is* the photograph, neatly illustrating Cartier-Bresson's concept of the 'decisive moment'. One second later, and the instant would be shattered:

> The girl clutches at the fence with her free hand, head back, back arched. The boy half rises out of his seat. A diner looks towards the two of them as if he is only just comprehending what the girl has been doing. And another diner turns towards the foreground, where a Ferrari loses its back end in a cloud of burning rubber.

(Blincoe and Thorne 2001: 18)

You will need a real photograph for this exercise – something you've found in a gallery, a book or magazine, or even one of the pictures you took in Activity 2. Your task is to describe what was happening just before the photograph was taken. Like Garland, you should use the present tense.

Activity 5   Writing through the senses

So far, you've experimented mainly with visual imagery. But the other senses are equally powerful, as we saw in Mansfield's use of physical sensations such as heat and cold. Use all of them – touch, taste, hearing, smell and vision. Here are some suggestions:

Food for thought

Even though the consumption of fast food and ready-cooked meals has been rising, TV chefs have never been more popular. Why? Because eating is a sensuous activity, and images of food are almost porno-graphic, a link cleverly exploited in Matthew Klam's story 'There Should Be a Name for It'. For this exercise, you need to go the nearest kitchen. There are all kinds of smells, sights, sounds, textures and, of course, tastes at your disposal, even in the most poorly stocked kitchen. But to keep matters simple, we'll just concentrate on any fruit and vegetables you find there. Study them just as carefully as you looked at the picture in the gallery. Compare the different yellows of lemons and bananas. Smell the earthy scent of potatoes. If all you have is a wizened old carrot from the back of the fridge, that will do. Think about how you'd describe its texture. Is it rubbery or dried up like an old Egyptian mummy? There's no need to do any writing at this stage. How would you describe a strawberry or a tomato to someone who's never tasted one?

Now cut the fruit and vegetables in half. Oranges, peppers and onions will release their scent. Look also at shapes and patterns – the filaments in a mushroom cap, the seeds in the apple core. Find ways of using all your senses – even hearing, which may not be so obvious. If you do have onions or mushrooms, fry them, noticing how they change in the process. Omnivores might like to try including meat in these activities. Have you ever looked closely at the textures of fat and muscle?

If you are a vegetarian, the very thought of handling raw meat might disgust you. There might be other types of food you find revolting – cabbage or rice pudding or even peanut butter. Both disgust and pleasure are heightened states of consciousness, accentuating your physical response. Write down descriptions of your favourite and most loathed foods, using the senses as fully as you can. Imagine your favourite food was suddenly unobtainable and you were trying to remember what it tasted like. The senses are all interconnected; the taste of an apple is inseparable from the smell and the crunch.

Shutting down the senses

Imagine that one of your senses, currently functioning, is gone. Describe how you would experience everyday activities – eating, drinking, having a bath. Concentrate on what does register or how sensations are changed, rather than on what is missing. It is quite common for one sense to compensate for another; blind people often have a keen sense of hearing. Reversing this activity, imagine you have all of the senses but one is especially acute, as strong as a dog's sense of smell or a bat's supersensitive hearing. I am especially interested in how you might respond to weather. Can you taste the rain? Does snow have a scent?

Last summer

Remember last summer? Thinking back quickly, jot down five sense impressions. You might be thinking of somewhere you spent a holiday or of the familiar things we associate with summer – lying on the beach, getting soaked in a storm or even sitting exams. Once you have noted these impressions, write a present-tense description of a moment from last summer. Take us there again, using all the senses. Looking back at Chekhov's comments in Activity 2, concentrate on conjuring up an atmosphere using small details.

Activity 6   Musical epiphanies

Music has a powerful impact on moods and feelings, as we saw in 'Morning Chemistry'. It can also transport you into the past; whenever I hear the saxophone riff from Gerry Rafferty's 'Baker Street' I am instantly back in that distant summer when I was a washer-up in a steak-house. Joyce makes many references to music in his stories, using them to usher in the epiphanies in 'Eveline' and 'The Dead'. Now you've had some practice in image-based writing, imagine another situation where a familiar song or a tune suddenly transports a character into the past. All that is necessary is the music and a basic idea of the character's situation. They could be someone looking back at their childhood or someone who is still quite young, perhaps recovering from a broken relationship. Write about 500 words in the third person, describing their intense reactions. Try and suggest how their state of mind has changed. What happens next?

Activity 7   Altered states

Using a 'stream of consciousness' technique, write as someone who is not in their normal state of mind – ill in bed, drunk, suffering from senile dementia or perhaps just very sleepy. Your character has an appointment somewhere, but cannot remember what it is. Write a first draft intensively, stopping after twenty minutes, then read it aloud. Compress and extend as necessary, aiming for a short short story (maximum 750 words), expressing the thoughts and feelings passing through your character's consciousness.

3

Humour

Comic effects go hand in hand with other aspects of storytelling. Humour surfaces in every type of story and in many different forms, from the gently ironic to the fiercely satirical. The English writer Molly Brown specializes in comic science fiction, while the American Elmore Leonard turns out crime capers. There are comic dimensions to almost any story. Samuel Beckett's pronouncements on futility, despair and death generate their own kind of bleak humour, a sly pessimism inherited by James Kelman. Humour often is in the eye of the beholder. The Argentinian critic Alberto Manguel says that his young daughter read Kafka's 'Metamorphosis' as a comic tale. (I discuss this story in the next chapter.) For many writers, humour is an optional extra; you can enjoy their work without necessarily understanding it at a comic level. But there are others whose prime aim is to tickle your funny bone. If you are not laughing, their story has fallen flat. This is the case with the core examples later in this chapter, the American Garrison Keillor and the Irishman Patrick McCabe.

In his introduction to a selection from P. G. Wodehouse, Hilaire Belloc stresses the precise craftsmanship of a writer whose stories, novels and journalism once epitomized English humour. He praises a 'simplicity and exactitude' which unfailingly delivers (Wodehouse 2003: 6). Like a cricket player or a violinist, Wodehouse makes his skills appear effortless. He simply has the knack for a certain type of comedy which still inspires a loyal readership, many years since its heyday in the 1930s.

This ability to make their work seem effortless is a gift that many comic writers share with stage performers. Truly great comedians can raise a laugh just by looking at the audience. They seem to have been born with that special nature, often projecting a childlike sense of mischief. This is certainly true of Wodehouse, whose stories are based on pranks and practical jokes; in 'Uncle Fred Flits By', for instance, the fun begins when Uncle Fred gains access to the house of a complete stranger by pretending he has come to clip the parrot's claws. Freud thought that jokes helped us regress to childhood. However, as the great British comedian Ken Dodd once said, Freud never played the Glasgow Empire. Philosophers may try to analyse humour, but they can never define its essence. Whether you're treading the boards or pounding the page, an innate talent still needs careful handling. As Belloc says, again of Wodehouse: 'The situation, the climax, general and particular, the interplay of character and circumstance are as exact as such arrangements can be. They produce the full effect and are always complete' (Wodehouse 2003: 7).

The lessons you learnt about structure and suspense in Chapter 1 can equally well be applied to building comic tension. Wodehouse piles on the laughs as relentlessly as Poe multiplies horror by horror until at the story's climax the ultimate absurdity is reached. Uncle Fred not only gets away with pretending to be the man to see the parrot but also manages to solve the problems of the household in a roundabout manner.

If you have a comic gift, you will never be short of a reader and this chapter will help you to make the most of your talents. Even if you are not quite so confident, humour can be developed from character observation, which I illustrate with examples from Elmore Leonard and Helen Simpson. Characterization largely depends on good dialogue, an essential for comedy writers and an important skill in other types of fiction. The concern with characterization and dialogue informs much of the chapter, including the activities at the end. The readings of Garrison Keillor and Patrick McCabe introduce distinctive types of parodic humour – the former through anecdotal writing and the latter using a fiercer, more satirical approach. Whether you are intending to produce specifically comic writing or not, this chapter should help you develop an authorial voice and work on character and dialogue. But I want to start with an elusive quality shared with both serious and comic writing – that concept known as 'irony'.

Irony

When I analysed 'Bliss' in the previous chapter, something I may not have made entirely clear was that Mansfield's story is meant to be funny. She sends up Bertha's pretensions. She exaggerates her supersensitivity so that it seems ridiculous. She also satirizes the poseurs at the dinner party:

> 'I have had such a *dreadful* experience with a taxi-man; he was *most* sinister. I couldn't get him to *stop*. The *more* I knocked and called the *faster* he went. And *in* the moonlight this *bizarre* figure with the *flattened* head crouching over the *lit-tle* wheel. . .'
>
> He shuddered, taking off an immense white silk scarf. Bertha noticed that his socks were white, too – most charming.
>
> (Mansfield 1984: 98)

Bertha's misreading of other people's motives generates a sense of irony when her rapport with Miss Fulton falls flat. Irony is one of the most subtle and productive effects at the writer's disposal. Because it is so delicate, it can be hard to define. Often it is achieved through understatement or silence. In another Mansfield story, 'Life of Ma Parker', irony arises from the gap between a young intellectual's preconceptions about his cleaning woman and the inner turmoil she is actually enduring after the death of her grandson. He regards her as rather a simpleton, but it is the urban sophisticate who appears the less complex character once her private thoughts are revealed, beneath the stoic exterior. We could try and define irony as just this gap between different streams of knowledge. The reader knows something the character doesn't, and the more oblivious they are, the deeper the irony. The New Testament saying 'What is a man profited, if he shall gain the whole world, and lose his own soul?' (Matthew 16: 26) might be regarded as an ironic statement.

The 'twist in the tale' is a popular device, not always handled with care. When it does succeed, it is often thanks to irony. In Margaret Yorke's 'The Reckoning', a long-suffering wife devises the perfect murder. All her machinations go to plan. In the full knowledge that her husband is lying dead in the cellar, she goes through her normal morning routine, preparing lunch as usual. As she smartens up at her dressing table, she is stung by a wasp in the hairbrush. Because of her own actions, there is no one in the house to save her from a fatal allergic reaction.

Both the biblical parable and the modern crime story depend on a clash between the character's expectations and the eventual outcome. In stories with a twist ending, the reader is as much in the dark as the character until the final page. When such stories fail, it is because the reader could see the twist coming or because the twist is just tacked on without any regard to logic or characterization. Roald Dahl's 'Lamb to the Slaughter' succeeds because it is psychologically plausible that a downtrodden wife should cook the frozen lamb she used to kill her husband and then serve it for the policemen's dinner. Unwittingly they consume vital evidence, never dreaming that the grieving widow is capable of murder. Irony lends a satisfying sense of balance and even a rough justice to Dahl's story and to Yorke's.

'The Reckoning' is a clever variation on two interrelated ideas. The first is that you get what you want only to discover it is worthless, the second that you are undone by your own actions. These concepts have a long storytelling history, reaching back deep into mythology. They are enacted in the legend of King Midas, whose touch turns everything to gold. The golden touch becomes the touch of death when his daughter runs heedlessly to greet him and is turned into a golden statue. By having his wishes granted he loses that which is most dear. King Midas's story is an instance of tragic irony. This should remind us how slight the division between comedy and tragedy can sometimes be.

Chekhov treads that thin line in his stories as well as in plays like *The Cherry Orchard*. 'The Bet' starts with a heated argument: which is worse, the death penalty or life imprisonment? To settle the debate, a young lawyer agrees to undertake fifteen years' solitary confinement for a vast sum of money. As the period nears its end, the banker who laid the bet is in reduced circumstances. To avoid financial ruin, he even contemplates killing his prisoner. But the lawyer has been changed by his years of study and contemplation. He is no longer interested in material wealth, and vanishes just before his time is up. The story is played out like an extended joke. The punchline consists of the final exchange of positions, the loser becoming the winner. But his victory is hollow. The suffering endured by both men gives the story a tragic weight, counterbalancing its inherent absurdity.

This ending achieves irony through plot reversal, a device we will encounter again in Maupassant's 'Country Living' (see Chapter 6). Irony also stems from incongruity – the policeman who is burgled, the doctor who falls ill. You can probably tell by the title that Elmore Leonard's 'How Carlos Webster Changed his Name to Carl and Became a Famous Oklahoma Lawman' is a deeply funny story (Chabon 2003). Carlos becomes a hero because he happens to be in the local drugstore buying an ice cream at the precise moment when two notorious robbers call by. Leonard spins out the story with the convoluted trail of circumstances leading up Carlos's almost incidental bravery. The comedy lies in the mundane – the sort of details that are left out of the legends that are told about him afterwards. We have to know that Carlos is purchasing two scoops of peach ice cream on a sugar cone and that outlaws are in the store to find Unguentine cream for a heat rash. Incongruity plays a part in almost every type of comedy. Leonard's story also depends on vivid characterization and dialogue, which we will look at more closely in the next section.

Character observation

One of the simplest approaches to comic writing is character observation. In Leonard's story, Carlos Webster begins as a polite, well-behaved fifteen-year-old whose apparent naivety turns out to be an asset in his adult career. The closing section of the story reaffirms his modesty as he sits with his father Virgil:

> They sat on the porch sipping tequila at the end of the day, insects out there singing in the dark. A lantern hung above Virgil's head so he could see to read the newspapers on his lap.
> 'Most of it seems to be what this little girl told.'
> 'They made up some of it.'
> 'Jesus, I hope so. You haven't been going out with her, have you?'
> 'I drove down, took her to Purity a couple times.'
> 'She's a pretty little thing. Has a saucy look about her in the pictures, wearing that kimona.'
> 'She smelled nice, too,' Carl said.
>
> (Chabon 2003: 122–3)

Writing sparely and simply, Leonard sketches in the scene with one or two details – the lantern, the insects 'singing'. He then lets character reveal itself through dialogue. Because we can hear those characters speaking we can also see them. Just reading the sentences makes me hear those Oklahoma voices without any need to use phonetic spelling, except in 'kimona'. The phrases and sentence structure – 'drove down, took her to Purity a couple times' – do the work for you.

This type of character portrait, structured around a turning point in that person's life, can also be used for a serious purpose. The Kenyan writer Ngũgĩ wa Thiong'o composed a series of 'secret lives', voicing experiences that are usually overlooked or ignored. In 'Minutes of Glory', a downtrodden bar-girl steals money from a man who has spent the night with her. She spends one whole day living it up before she is arrested. Most of the story describes her daily existence up to this point, just as Leonard's story is filled with the background to Carlos's transformation into Carl the lawman. Some of the activities at the end of the chapter will explore ways of fleshing out a character study into a substantial story.

The British writer Helen Simpson deals wittily with the lives of educated women who have sacrificed their independence in return for motherhood and marriage. Her sardonic sense of humour brings out the absurdity in the rituals of modern life. In 'Hurrah for the Hols', her protagonist, Dorrie, witnesses a man at the next table trying to force a burger down an unwilling child:

> 'If you don't do what I say right now there'll be no ice cream. No swimming. No puppet show. I mean it.'
>
> The small boy beside him started to cry into his burger, wailing and complaining that his teeth hurt.
>
> 'And don't think you're going to get round me like that,' snarled the man. 'I'm not your *mother*, remember!'
>
> (Simpson 2001: 161)

Many of us will have witnessed a scene like that – and even recorded it in our notebooks. Watching the incident, Dorrie is fully aware that she herself is capable of equally unreasonable behaviour. She is on a typically British seaside holiday, trying to keep the family occupied and spend some time with Max, her husband. Simpson exposes the unwritten laws of family life. Even the children's quarrels seem precisely choreographed:

> Maxine had been trying to pull her bag of crisps away from Martin, who had suddenly let go, with the result that Maxine's

crisps had flown into the air and over the grass, where Martin was now rolling on them and crushing them into salty fragments.

'Stop it!' called Dorrie.

'Get up this minute!' shouted Max.

'Why should I, it's a free country,' gabbled Martin, rolling back and forth, enjoying the noise and drama.

(Simpson 2001: 167–8)

Everyone is fulfilling a set role in the family melodrama. Martin parrots an adult cliché; lots of the things we do and say almost automatically are actually meaningless. Every social group – not just families – takes certain sorts of behaviour for granted which seem weird or ridiculous if you stop to think about them. Think about the unwritten rules you are forced to negotiate if you start a new school or college. Simpson takes an ordinary situation and builds a story out of small incidents. Not all of them are fraught with tension. There are moments of pure pleasure – a shared joke or the sight of a shimmering dragonfly. Life is not a bed of roses, but there are compensations, and in the end we just have to get on with it. In the closing pages the mood changes as Dorrie manages to get out on a solitary walk across the beach. The story moves away from social comedy, exploring her state of mind at a much deeper level, using the imagery of the landscape and the sound of an unknown child wailing in the distance.

By making us laugh, Simpson can make serious points without appearing to have an axe to grind. It also removes the risk of sentimentality in her portrayal of children. Essentially, 'Hurrah for the Hols' is strung together from a series of disconnected incidents. In that sense, you could say it is closer to the image-based fiction of Katherine Mansfield than to comic writers like Wodehouse. Rather than piling on increasing chaos, Simpson finishes with an open, ambiguous ending. Simpson's story illustrates one approach to building fiction from character observation, linking random incidents together in the framework of a family holiday. With the concept of the 'anecdote', I switch my attention to small-town humour and the development of a comic voice.

The anecdote: 'News' (Garrison Keillor, 1985)

In 'How to Tell a Story', Mark Twain enlarges on the art of telling a humorous story. The humorous story, as opposed to 'comic' or 'witty' stories, is an American oral tradition, disjointed and rambling and told with a straight face. 'The humorous story may be spun out to great length, and may wander around as much as it pleases, and arrive at nowhere in particular' (Twain 2000: 235). Despite the laid-back attitude, Twain goes on to discuss, once again, the importance of timing, describing a vital pause at the climax of a story he told at public readings.

Twain popularized this deadpan tradition, merging fiction, journalism, autobiographical sketches and monologues – a tradition upheld by later writers such as James Thurber and, more recently, Garrison Keillor. Keillor's Lake Wobegon stories began as broadcasts on Minnesota Public Radio. In between records, he would tell anecdotes which became monologues, and eventually these were incorporated into a show called *A Prairie Home Companion. A Prairie Home Companion* still goes out weekly, mixing words, music and Keillor's twenty-minute monologue, *The News from Lake Wobegon*. Although the programme is still broadcast from Minnesota, for much of the year it goes on the road. An even wider audience access the programme via the Internet on <http://www.prairiehome.org> (accessed 25 July 2004).

Keillor freely admits that his writing is loosely based on his own experiences. Why make it up when there is all that material right under your nose? The fictional Lake Wobegon embodies the mid-western culture he grew up in. Keillor achieves his comic effects by embellishing and exaggerating its characteristics. Not everything he describes really happened, but when we read his stories we believe it could have.

Easygoing and circuitous, the Lake Wobegon stories fit Twain's definition of the 'humorous story' perfectly. 'News' begins as an informative account of the local newspaper, but almost immediately starts to digress:

> The Lake Wobegon *Herald-Star* (formerly the *Star*, then the *Sun*, then bought by Harold Starr in 1944) is published every Tuesday and mailed second-class to some fifteen hundred subscribers, most of whom don't live there anymore (and wouldn't if you paid them) but who shell out $30 a year to read about it.
>
> (Keillor 1988: 250)

The parentheses – two pairs of brackets in the first sentence – are warning signs. Keillor will not stay on any single point but will, as Twain put it, 'wander around' as he pleases. The story is a miscellany of local gossip. It soon emerges that what the paper doesn't contain, amongst the minutiae of weddings and ball games, is the real news, the story behind the story:

> It wasn't news that Ruthie and Bob got married, marriage was more or less inevitable under the circumstances; the *news* was the miracle of architecture Mrs. Mueller worked on Ruthie's dress, making it look flat in front, and then, six months later, the baby boy – not *out* of wedlock, but not quite far enough *into* wedlock either.
>
> (Keillor 1988: 256)

Keillor writes in a conversational style, forging a bond with the reader. Like a stand-up comedian, he knows how appear improvisational while staying firmly in control. At the end of a digression, he often doubles back on himself to fill in a gap in the narrative:

> When I say 'my mother,' I mean the woman who raised me – my real mother was in the carnival, she was the fat lady and the tight-rope walker, and I was born during an outdoor show – she thought it was some pancakes she ate, and there she was fifty-seven feet in the air over the Mississippi River, she dropped the balancing pole and she caught me by the ankle as I fell – I still have a mark there – and somehow she made it to the other side and handed me down to the man who ran the cotton-candy stand and said, 'Here. Take care of this for me, willya?'
>
> (Keillor 1988: 262)

This tall tale may strain credibility, but for the most part the picture of small-town life seems fully authentic. Anecdotal humour is a kind of public performance. Keillor constructs a version of himself, a storytelling voice. He even includes a newspaper article about himself:

> Mr Gary Keillor visited at the home of Al and Florence Crandall on Monday and after lunch returned to St. Paul, where he is currently employed in the radio show business. Mr Lew Powell also visited, who recently

> celebrated his ninety-third birthday and is
> enjoying excellent health. Almost twelve
> quarts of string beans were picked and some
> strawberries. Lunch was fried chicken with
> gravy and creamed peas.
>
> (Keillor 1988: 272–3)

Maintaining the illusion, Keillor even comments on the piece, allegedly written by Florence, his aunt, in person, 'and the careful reader can see that she still dotes on her wayward nephew, pointing out his gainful and glamorous employment and suggesting that he is no slouch on a bean row, either, giving a little plug for family longevity and complimenting the guests with a good lunch' (Keillor 1988: 273). Keillor knows mid-western culture inside out. The reader trusts him because the language and the characters are observed accurately. The story appeals to mid-westerners who enjoy acknowledging their own cultural foibles. But a national and even a global readership can also identify with the characters. In a copious footnote, running the length of the story, he lays out '95 Theses' allegedly composed by a Wobegonian with a grudge against his parents. The theses list the inbred attitudes its writer has struggled to resist:

> 21. Suffering was its own reward, to be preferred to pleasure. As Lutherans, we viewed pleasure with suspicion. Birth control was never an issue with us. Nor was renunciation of pleasures of the flesh. We never enjoyed them in the first place.
>
> (Keillor 1988: 259)

The stubborn stoicism and the guilt and fatalism he associates with Protestantism are fairly widespread elsewhere in other Anglo-Saxon cultures, throughout the world. British readers took instantly to *Lake Wobegon Days*, making it a best-seller in that country too. By describing a very specific geographical location, Keillor produces a vivid piece of writing with a potential readership extending far beyond that neighbourhood.

Introducing a more cynical note, the *95 Theses* undercut any folksiness in the main text. Keillor likes fragmenting the narrative in this way. The recipes, poems, songs, school handouts and other additions to his stories add to the impression that he is merely collecting snippets of local history. 'News' is all about storytelling in that it explores the ways in which gossip and local legends travel around a community. Lake Wobegon may be far removed from your own environment, but you only have to go down to your nearest shop or listen in on a phone conversation to tap into a bottomless reservoir of stories.

Parody and satire: 'The Hands of Dingo Deery' (Patrick McCabe, 1999)

Patrick McCabe also chronicles provincial life, drawing on material from his own background in the Irish midlands. But his view of the world is far harsher than Keillor's: 'Being born, living and dying', he says '– it is mayhem, chaos and madness' (O'Mahony 2003). His collection *Mondo Desperado* takes its title from the 'shockumentaries' of the 1960s and 1970s – films with titles like *Mondo Bizarro*, *Mondo Freudo* and *Sexy Magico*. McCabe's own style has been called 'bog Gothic'. He revels in the savagely grotesque, using gross physical humour. Where Keillor seems to be speaking personally, McCabe dons a more obvious mask, speaking through first-person narrators who verge on the insane. They are instances of the 'unreliable narrator', whose version of events should not be taken at face value.

'The Hands of Dingo Deery' parodies the tale of mystery and suspense. It mimics the strategies used by writers like Poe and Lovecraft to build up suspense, foreshadowing unspeakable horrors in its opening paragraph: 'How many years have I paced these accursed floorboards, imploring any deity who cares to listen to return to me the bountiful tranquillity which once was mine and end for ever this dread torment which greets me like a rapacious shade each waking day!' (McCabe 1999: 75).

The narrator, Dermot Mooney, recalls his boyhood, thirty years ago, describing his summers in the town of Barntrosna, where his uncle, Louis Lestrange, was a headmaster. McCabe subverts the language of nostalgia, randomly yoking symbols from the glorious past and the tainted present: 'Yuri Gagarin was in space, Player's cost one and six and John Fitzgerald Kennedy was undoubtedly the possessor of the cleanest teeth in the Western hemisphere. It was to be many years before the arrival of colour television and the first drug addicts' (McCabe 1999: 77–8).

As so often in comic writing, humour stems from the incongruous. The over-inflated style collides with the banality of the subject matter. An ordinary cup of tea becomes 'the soothing, tan-coloured liquid' (McCabe 1999: 83). Mooney's drunken binge is described as giving himself 'to the arms of Bacchus' (McCabe 1999: 84). Conscious of the disparity between his fevered visions and mundane reality, the reader sees through his naïve interpretation of events as they unfold.

Mooney spends long hours at a local café, the Pronto Grill, admiring the convent girls 'who would converge there in the afternoons, rapt in their sophistry and circumscribing elongated shapes in the spilt sugar' (McCabe 1999: 83). His fantasies are shattered when the girls are joined by Dingo Deery. Deery is an ex-pupil and 'well-known layabout' (McCabe 1999: 77) who has often disturbed his uncle's public lectures on bird-watching with threats and recriminations: 'You think he knows about birds? He knows nothing! Except how to beat up poor unfortunate scholars for not knowing their algebra! Look at these hands! Look at them, damn youse!' (McCabe 1999: 77). Deery's hands are marked by scars from schoolroom beatings.

Mooney's uncle has started to act rather strangely, amongst other things disappearing for long stretches during the night. Mooney starts keeping watch, and when he sees Lestrange entering the woods with his binoculars he is convinced that he is doing some nocturnal bird-watching. In fact, he is spying on the convent girls, who are shooting porno films with Dingo Deery. When he captures the boy and his uncle Deery has his revenge by forcing them both to perform on camera. He takes particular delight in filming Lestrange being caned by the girls. These are the memories which torture poor Mooney and have driven him to exile in a dingy London bedsitter. Even now from his window he can see the letters spelt out on the front of a cinema: 'THE SECRETS OF LOUIS LESTRANGE: CAN YOU SURVIVE THE 1,137 WHACKS?' (McCabe 1999: 75).

McCabe spent his boyhood immersed in the *Dandy*, *Hotspur* and Marvel comics. The comic-book influence is very apparent, especially in his characterization. The pornographer Mick Macardle, who passes the films on to his contacts in Amsterdam, is a caricature, with his slicked-back hair and dark moustache. Macardle and Deery do not merely speak. They 'snarl', 'snap' and 'snicker' like comic-book villains. The film director and writer Ethan Coen also uses comic-book hoodlums in stories like 'Cosa Minopalidan' which parody hard-boiled detective fiction. Writers can have a lot of fun exploiting familiar conventions.

Yet despite this debt to popular fiction, McCabe's sardonic vision does have a basis in reality. Like Garrison Keillor – and, of course, Helen Simpson – he makes us see the bizarre nature of ordinary social rituals:

The church bells would ring out across the morning town, the womenfolk give themselves once more to the fastidious investigation of vegetables and assorted foodstuffs in the grocery halls, brightening each other's lives with picturesque travelogues of failing innards and the more recent natural disasters, delaying perhaps at the corner to engage in lengthy discourse with Fr. Dominic, their beloved pastor. 'That's not a bad day now,' they would observe, the clergyman as a rule finding himself in fulsome agreement. 'Indeed and it is not,' he would respond enthusiastically, occasionally a dark cloud of uncertainty passing across his fresh, close-shaven features as he added: 'Although I think we might get a touch of rain later!'

(McCabe 1999: 79–80)

Like the other writers we have mentioned, he uses snatches of dialogue to animate his characters. Once again, turns of phrase and sentence structure suggest local speech, including accent.

McCabe is a more markedly satirical writer than Keillor, demonstrating little affection for his characters. Satire mocks the most degenerate aspects of current society and human vice. It is usually politically subversive, like Swift's eighteenth-century essay 'A Modest Proposal', which advocated that the starving Irish fatten their children for the English table. In stories like 'Sugar Baby' and 'Girls at War', the Nigerian Chinua Achebe deals with the corrupting effects of war and deprivation through characters who will do anything to get hold of scarce commodities. Underneath the comic anarchy, 'The Hands of Dingo Deery' exposes a seamy side to Irish life at odds with conventional images of the Emerald Isle.

Satire operates through negativity. You are presenting what you disapprove of without overt criticism, let alone offering any sort of alternative. Readers can draw their own conclusion. George Saunders's 'I Can Speak!™' is a fictional letter from a representative of 'KidLuv, Inc.', replying to a customer complaint about its product. The I Can Speak!™ is 'an innovative and essential educational tool that, used with proper parental guidance, offers a rare early development opportunity for babies and toddlers alike' (Cassini and Testa 2003: 3). Although the narrator is reluctant to use the word 'mask', the product fits over the child's face giving the illusion of speech:

Sometimes we have felt that our childless friends think badly of us for having a kid who just goes glub glub glub in the corner while looking at his feces on his thumb. But now when childless friends are over, what we have found, my wife, Ann, and I, is that it's great to have your kid say something witty and self-possessed years before he or she would actually in reality be able to say something witty or self-possessed. The bottom line is that it's just *fun* when you and your childless friends are playing cards, and your baby suddenly blurts out (in his *very own probable future voice*), 'IT IS LIKELY THAT WE STILL DON'T FULLY UNDERSTAND THE IMPORT OF ALL EINSTEIN'S FINDINGS!'

(Cassini and Testa 2003: 6)

The convoluted prose mimics self-satisfied corporate speech. Saunders satirizes middle-class attitudes towards child-rearing in a consumer culture. Although, thankfully, the I Can Speak!™ may be some way off, some parents do display their offspring like fashion accessories. Anticipating the fads of the future leads us into the territory of science fiction, but, as we have seen, there is enough eccentricity in present-day reality to keep us plentifully supplied with comic and satiric material.

Humour, as Twain recognized, should not be forced. There's no need to strain for effect by labouring obvious jokes. Most of the humour in this chapter, even the most surreal, has been rooted in observation and characterization. Once you have started listening and taking note the comedy reveals itself. The activities that follow will help you tune into the comedy wavelength. They will also build skills in characterization and dialogue and in the development of a confident authorial voice.

Activity 1　Voice

Garrison Keillor is the man who wrote *Lake Wobegon Days*. He was born in Anoka, Minnesota, in 1942, and is remembered by his classmates as rather shy and bookish. 'Garrison Keillor' is also the fictional character who helped pick almost twelve quarts of beans. Then there is a third personality, largely coinciding with that second incarnation – the authorial presence addressing the reader. I began this book by emphasizing the importance of a compelling narrative voice in storytelling. Keillor speaks directly to his audience in a literal sense on the airwaves, but all good writers, whether we are aware of it or not, establish a bond with their readers by sustaining a distinctive narrative voice.

As a new writer, you may take some time to find that voice. While you're learning your craft, you may find yourself unconsciously picking up linguistic habits from the writers you are reading. So long as you are not just blindly copying, that doesn't matter. Those writers themselves will have borrowed from their predecessors. As you gain in confidence, your own voice will emerge. That voice will be pitched slightly differently, according to the piece you are writing. For many writers, finding the right voice is the key to getting started on a tale they want to tell. You might think of it as tuning an instrument before you start playing. The Canadian Mavis Gallant has spoken about worrying away at the very first sentence before she can go any further. I suspect this is at least partially connected with this question of voice.

Your writing voice will derive largely from your speaking voice. It should feel natural to you. Forget any pressure to write 'standard' or 'good' English. When writing academic essays, you are encouraged to write impersonally, but when you are writing creatively you are writing as yourself. Your writing personality may be slightly different to your usual character, but it is still shaped by your own background and outlook. Garrison Keillor writes with a mid-western drawl.

To develop your own voice, write a 250-word monologue. Keep it light-hearted, but don't worry about making it sound funny. Here are some possible topics:

- the opposite sex
- the worst thing about Christmas
- if I could change the law
- my most embarrassing moment
- my idea of paradise
- my idea of hell.

Anything you love or loathe can provide material for a monologue – sport, music, movie stars, the US President . . . If the feelings come through, then the writer's voice makes itself present. As you can see from my suggestions, a contrary attitude tends to be the most fertile. Even if you love Christmas, the things that go wrong or annoy you are the things that will spice up your writing, and – who knows? – generate comedy. When you have finished the monologue, read it aloud to yourself. Then edit the piece, paring down and intensifying the language. Don't build up to the topic; get straight in there from the start. Make sure you end forcefully.

Activity 2   Another monologue

Your second monologue will be longer, between 500 and 1000 words. This time your title begins with the words 'How to . . .' Mark Twain's sketch 'How I Edited an Agricultural Paper' is a typical piece of anecdotal writing. John Updike's 'How to Love America and Leave it at the Same Time' is a fully fledged short story, developing a set of instructions into a jaundiced portrayal of family life in modern America, 'a hamburger kingdom, one cuisine, under God, indivisible, with pickles and potato chips for all' (Updike 2004: 414).

Consider developing these monologues into longer stories. You could add one or several anecdotes illustrating your argument; or expand something you've already included, adding dialogue and description. Reading your work aloud is always useful whenever you're redrafting. Hearing how the words sound detaches you slightly from your writing, making it easier to edit. You can also sense the rhythms of the language and test out your writing voice. This is a point we will come back to in the redrafting checklist at the end of the book.

Activity 3   Larger than life

He was ten years old when I knew him. He was a Hammer of God, defying not Rome or the crown but the Hebrew school principal. His name was Michael Simkin. Like the great scourges of history – Genghis Khan, Oliver Cromwell, Omar Mukhtar – he seemed invulnerable, in his case perhaps because he was too young to execute. Or so we believed.

(Coen 1999: 43)

Think of someone you have known who seems larger than life. It could be someone fairly familiar like the classmate in Coen's story or an eccentric you've watched from a distance; Candida Clark's 'Mr Miller' (Blincoe and Thorne 2001) is a foul-mouthed drunk muttering to himself in a bar.

Imagine this person is missing. Using their own name or one you've invented, write a short description – no more than 100 words – which would make them instantly recognizable.

The things that mark out an individual, in fiction or real life, are not their passport details. The colour of their hair or their eyes or their height in metres may be irrelevant. When you can't be with a loved one the things you miss about them may be the sound of their voice or a smell or a gesture. The essence of a character is conveyed by these small details rather than a full physical description. Even a caricatured figure such as McCabe's Mick Macardle is defined by his cigar and moustache. In 'News', we hear all about Harold Starr's toupee, which tends to slip forwards.

Starting from the details in your original description, complete a character sketch of about 1000 words. Feel free to invent and embellish. Comic effects are not obligatory, though you may include them if you wish. It is important to set your characters in motion. What do they do, where do they go, what are their secrets? What is their greatest desire? These are the things you can only guess at and as you write you will necessarily speculate. This in turn will start transforming your character into fiction. If you know their real name, change it. Change one other detail from the original description.

Activity 4 Lonely hearts

'Likes Greek islands, cartooning and ghost-busting' – 'Hippy 54 and house that time forgot' – 'Not all rashes are nervous. Find out how'. People advertising for a date try to give clues to themselves, or at least to the personalities they'd like to project. Ignoring the duller details – 'slim', 'good sense of humour' etc. – write another character sketch based on one of these adverts, from a publication or Internet source of your choice. There are plenty out there, and plenty of single people of all ages and all walks of life. You need not mention the advertisement or why they are looking for a partner. The aim is to use the details they supply as ingredients for a fictional character.

The fifty-four-year-old hippy has realized that characters are largely defined by their natural habitat. His house says as much about him as his age or appearance. Picture the person at home. Think of Carl on the porch in Elmore Leonard's story or the lonely bedsit where Patrick McCabe's Dermot Mooney treads the 'accursed floorboards'. When you have finished this activity, take a look at 'Love Story', by the American Caren Gussoff, a comic parody which merges the lonely hearts column with a job application (Prior 2003).

Activity 5   Names

I hope you gave your character a name in the previous exercise. Names communicate information about a character instantly. Garrison Keillor only needs to namecheck 'Carl Krebsbach's cousin Ernie Barnecht, No-Neck Ernie' to put us in the picture (Keillor 1988: 261). Patrick McCabe specializes in outlandish names: Dingo Deery, Louis Lestrange. Dermot Mooney's name is more ordinary but it sums him up perfectly by suggesting his habit of mooning around the convent girls at the Pronto Grill – not to mention his uncle's 'elderly moons' when he is beaten for the camera (McCabe 1999: 91). Ethan Coen calls his character 'Michael Simkin' precisely because it sounds totally innocuous.

For this exercise, you need to find a partner. Over a couple of days, you should collect a variety of names. Newspapers are a good source, and so are the credits at the end of television programmes. Try using the real names of Hollywood actors; Cary Grant changed his name from the more homely Archibald Leach. Some names like 'Archibald Leach' stand out because they sound old-fashioned and down to earth, others because they're exotic. Select half a dozen or so and write each name on a slip of paper. Then swap with your partner. Take a lucky dip and jot down some notes on the character you have picked at random.

Now you and your partner will interview each other for a maximum of ten minutes each. Once you have established the basics, such as job, age and marital status, try to get a little more in depth with more detailed or personal questions. What kind of car do they drive? Have they ever been in love? What did they have for breakfast? When you are being inter-viewed you *are* that character. Don't be put off if some questions are difficult to answer. Just take your time and stay in character. Ten minutes is longer than you think. Once you have completed the interviews, write a monologue in which your character introduces her/himself.

The English writer E. M. Forster made a useful distinction between 'flat' and 'round' characters in fiction. When you create a 'round' char-acter, you give them psychological depth, along with the ability to mature and change. These are the sorts of characters who are said to take on a life of their own, who writers often claim have simply run away with them. By and large, I have encouraged you to develop this type of character in these exercises on character observation. One of the reasons I have asked you to work intuitively is that I want to leave room for quirks and contradictions. People do have unpredictable sides to their nature. But a 'flat' character, who is fixed and one-dimensional like a cartoon, is equally valid, especially in comic writing. Patrick McCabe's characters are 'flat', and so is Ethan Coen's Michael Simkin. They embody particular characteristics. There might have been other badly behaved children, but Michael Simkin was disruption personified, just as Dingo Deery embodied everything that Dermot Mooney despised. Consider whether the characters you have invented are 'round' or 'flat'. We will come back to 'flat' characterization in Activity 8.

Activity 6   Dialogue

As we saw in the extract from Elmore Leonard, dialogue reveals character. Leonard is rightly regarded as a master of sharp, punchy dialogue. Good dialogue rings true. Listen to the voices all around you, and even write down the choicest expressions; think of the children fighting in Helen Simpson's story or the women shopping in 'The Hands of Dingo Deery' or Katherine Mansfield's snob who had 'such a *dreadful* experience'. Start taking the bus – much better for eaves-dropping than sitting alone in a car. The Indian writer R. K. Narayan was inspired to write 'The Shelter' after overhearing a couple whispering on a bus.

Getting the dialogue right is one of the trickiest aspects of fiction, and another good reason for reading your stories out loud. Making up a conversation between the characters becomes less daunting when you consider it as one step up from the monologues which you have already practised. How often do we really listen to what the other person is saying? In 'News', the narrator describes a phone conversation with his old Sunday-school teacher. She starts to lecture him on his shortcomings until he prompts her for memories of his grandpa. Every time they go through the same routine.

Most dialogue is a stylized rendition of everyday speech. It keeps enough repetitions, hesitations, interruptions and rambling to sound true to life, without getting too bogged down. Although some stories are told almost entirely in dialogue, it often works best when kept to a minimum. The dialogue gives samples of conversation, in fragments rather than chunks. The following suggestions are designed to broaden your awareness of different types of speech and to ease you into using dialogue in your work. In long exchanges, there is no need to keep repeating 'he said' or 'she said' if it is clear who is speaking. Avoid adverbs, for example, 'she said bitterly', 'he said tenderly'. The dialogue itself should communicate the tone in which the words are said.

My mother said

In the *95 Theses* ('News'), the former Wobegonian quotes his parents' favourite expressions back at them: – 'When the going gets tough, the tough get going' (Keillor 1988: 256), 'Oh, never mind. I'll do it myself' (Keillor 1998: 272), 'Can't you walk without sounding like a herd of elephants?' (Keillor 1998: 274). List your own family expressions.

Terms of endearment, terms of abuse

Everybody has an individual language, influenced by their culture and background and personal idiosyncrasies. Do you say 'goodbye', 'ciao' or 'see you later?' What do you say when you answer the phone? In Matthew Klam's 'There Should be a Name for It', the narrator's girlfriend calls him 'Termite' (Cassini and Testa 2003: 15) while her mother says he is a 'goddamn jackass' (Cassini and Testa 2003: 16). List the names you call those close to you – whether your boyfriend or girlfriend, your dog or your grandmother. There are shades of difference 'Granny', 'Grandma' and 'Nan'. And what do they call you? Then make a list of the names you give people who annoy you – especially strangers. What do you yell at a roadhog? There should be some colourful language.

Mobile

Mobile phones are a gift for the dedicated people-watcher. Their owners often speak loudly without inhibitions as if no one else could hear them. Write a short piece (up to 1000 words) based on a mobile-phone conversation. It should be obvious that the person making the call is lying about where they really are. You can include one or both sides of the dialogue; it also up to you whether you include description or rely on speech entirely.

Reunited

Two characters who have not seen each for years meet again by chance. It is entirely up to you how well they knew one another, why they haven't met since then or how they bump into each other. They could be old schoolfriends, ex-lovers or even members of the same family. Do they both recognize each other? Are they pleased to meet again? If there is unfinished business between them, they may not refer to it explicitly; could you suggest any underlying tensions through dialogue? Write down what they say to each other.

Activity 7   Social comedy

Having completed the work on dialogue and character, you are going to explore different types of comic writing for the rest of the activities. As I have already stressed, don't force the humour; especially in this first exercise, it should emerge from the material.

Writing from different sides of the Atlantic, Patrick McCabe and Garrison Keillor both play on small-town humour. They see the absurdities of their own culture. Katherine Mansfield mocks London sophisticates, while Helen Simpson sees the funny side of contemporary middle-class families. They have all used places and social groupings known to them intimately. Their characters are recognizable types, composites of the priests or farmers, aesthetes or small children inhabiting a narrow milieu.

Passing fads are a good source of material – followed slavishly while they're in style, then seeming ludicrous once they're outmoded. In 'Bernice Bobs her Hair', F. Scott Fitzgerald's protagonist succumbs to the 1920s craze for short hair, instantly regretting her decision. Write a story about a character whose life is changed, for better or worse, by a fad or a cult. They might be a fashion victim or they might follow alternative medicine. There are trends in sport, in books – even in religions. Just look at the 'in' and 'out' columns in style magazines. Like the writers we've examined, set your story in a world you know well.

Activity 8   Parody

Parody is one of the most common tools used by the writers in this chapter. Parody exaggerates a set of conventions in order to poke fun at them. Keillor parodies local newspapers; McCabe parodies tales of mystery and suspense and comic books; George Saunders parodies corporate language with the I Can Speak!™. Characters in a parody tend to be 'flat' rather than round, and the language is pushed to an extreme.

Write your own parody of a magazine article. Choose anything you like from any kind of magazine or newspaper – an interview from the music press, an agony column, travel advice or the sports page. Choose something you would read yourself; it is better to relax into a style you already know well than to be too analytical about this exercise.

Another idea is to parody one of the other genres discussed in this book – the horror story for instance, or science fiction. There is no better way of paying tribute to a genre you enjoy.

Activity 9   Pranks

This final exercise is an excuse to be silly. The perpetrator must be someone who is, like Wodehouse's Uncle Fred, completely irresponsible and probably worthless. But, even if it threatens to go wrong, he or she must get away with it. Include all of these ingredients:

• disguise or mistaken identity
• a large sum of money or a valuable object
• an animal
• a mode of transport (car, train, bike, plane – whatever)
• an authority figure (schoolteacher, doctor, officer of the law, stern relative).

I hope you've enjoyed exploring humour in your writing. If you want to continue with comic writing, you can incorporate humour into most of the exercises in future chapters. It may be that you won't be able to resist.

4

The fantastic

Voluntary dreams

Every story is, to some extent, a fantasy. Even if your fiction is based very closely on real events, it has been filtered through your own distinctive mentality. In an essay about Kafka, whose work we discuss in this chapter, the Russian-born writer Nabokov imagines three individuals walking through a landscape. One is from the city, on holiday, one is a botanist and one is a local farmer. The first will see some picturesque greenery and a road leading to a restaurant. The second is able to look much more closely at nature; 'to him the world of the stolid tourist (who cannot distinguish an oak from an elm) seems a fantastic, vague, dreamy, never-never world' (Nabokov 1980: 252). But the farmer's perceptions outdo both these limited sets of responses, for 'his world is intensely emotional and personal since he has been born and bred there, and knows every trail and individual tree, and every shadow from every tree across every trail, all in warm connection with his everyday work, and his childhood, and a thousand small things and patterns which the other two – the humdrum tourist and the botanical taxonomist – simply cannot know in the given place at the given time' (Nabokov 1980: 253).

Of course all three versions would be different again if each of the characters was remembering the landscape, rather than just walking through it. These are the kind of issues we talked about in Chapter 2, when we explored ways of capturing subjective experience. Nabokov's point is that the distinction between fantasy and reality is a false one. Borges, whose work we discuss later, said that all artistic creation means surrendering ourselves to a 'voluntary dream' (Borges 1971: 220).

Within that dream, there are storytellers who set out to deliberately flout the laws of nature – writers who invent a reality separated from the everyday world. Many write science fiction, which we look at more closely in Chapter 5. In this chapter, I'm going to outline three different approaches to the fantastic. The first involves the transformation of everyday life by a single, extraordinary event, the second is based on myth and the third requires the creation of an alternative universe. My first main example will be the German-speaking Czech Franz Kafka's long story 'Metamorphosis' (I am keeping its more familiar title, although the translation I refer to calls it 'The Transformation'). The second approach is illustrated by the British writer Angela Carter's 'The Company of Wolves'; and the third relates to the Argentinian Jorge Luis Borges's 'Tlön, Uqbar, Orbis Tertius'. These three approaches do not, by any means, exhaust the possibilities, but they do suggest techniques you can adopt yourself. Fantasy, or 'magic realism' as it is sometimes known, is exciting for both the reader and the writer. It liberates the imagination, conferring absolute power to change or invent reality.

Altering reality: 'Metamorphosis' (Franz Kafka, 1915)

Gregor Samsa is a travelling salesman, living with his family in Prague. One morning he wakes up to find himself turned into a giant insect:

> He was lying on his hard shell-like back and by lifting his head a little he could see his curved brown belly, divided by stiff arching ribs, on top of which the bed-quilt was precariously poised and seemed about to slide off completely. His numerous legs, which were pathetically thin compared to the rest of his bulk, danced helplessly before his eyes.
>
> (Kafka 1992: 76)

Gregor has been dreaming, but this is no nightmare. Kafka describes the very real physical difficulties Gregor faces. Thinking it best just to go back to sleep, he tries shifting onto his right side, but his new body makes it impossible to get into his usual position. Lying awake, he runs through his other problems – the boss, financial difficulties, train connections – until he realizes he's overslept.

Being late for work seems to bother him much more than the transformation. After the initial panic, Gregor tries to stay calm. But even getting out of bed demands enormous physical effort, and when he finally lands on the floor he hurts himself quite badly. Meanwhile, his parents are hanging round the door, joined by an angry chief clerk from the office. Gregor decides to give them what they all want. He opens the door: 'If they took fright, then Gregor would have no further responsibility and could rest in peace. But if they took it all calmly, then he had no reason to get excited either, and he could, if he hurried, actually be at the station by eight' (Kafka 1992: 85).

Apart from the one important change, nothing out of the ordinary is happening at this point. Gregor could be any office worker, secretly raging against his boss, bowed down by money troubles, going through the daily grind. Nowhere in the story is there any attempt to explain Gregor's predicament. In down-to-earth language, the narrative records his actions, following the logic of the situation. Kafka explains exactly how an insect might turn the key in a door, sparing none of the discomfort Gregor endures in the process. The reactions when he does succeed, revealing himself to those waiting outside, are seen as if through a camera's eye: 'his father clenched a fist with a menacing expression, as if he meant to beat Gregor back into his own room, then he looked uncertainly round the living-room, covered his eyes with his hands and fell into a sobbing that shook his mighty chest' (Kafka 1992: 87). This dispassionate 'camera's eye' is also turned on the family apartment: 'the door leading to the hall was open, and since the front door of the flat was open too, it was possible to see out to the landing and the top of the stairs going down' (Kafka 1992: 87).

Gregor's father drives him violently into his room, where he stays imprisoned for most of the story. While Gregor's human instincts are gradually subsumed by insect characteristics, the family copes as best it can. Although Gregor thinks he is talking, they cannot understand him. When his sister puts down a saucer of bread and milk, he finds himself disgusted by human food. She quickly works out that he is far happier with the family leftovers and rotting vegetables. It is Gregor's sister who assumes responsibility for him, but eventually her compassion turns to revulsion. The whole family is mortified by this creature who, neglected and weakened by injuries – most of them inflicted by the Samsas – willingly lets himself die.

This brief summary leaves out the elaborate details given by Kafka. The narrative unfolds almost in slow motion as Kafka gives his painstaking account of Gregor's decline. His laborious movements, his thought processes and the nuances of the family's response are carefully rendered. For instance, Gregor manages to push an armchair up to the window so he can look out. Noticing this, his sister starts to leave it there for him, but when, arriving early, she catches sight of him, she runs away in horror. Realizing that even hiding under the sofa might not be enough for her, he takes further precautions:

> In order to spare her even this sight, he one day transported a sheet to the sofa on his back – the task took him four hours – and arranged it in such a way that he was now completely covered, and his sister would not be able to see him even if she stooped down. If she had considered this sheet unnecessary, then of course she could have removed it, for it was clear enough that Gregor was hardly shutting himself off so completely for his own amusement, but she left the sheet where it was, and Gregor even fancied that he had once caught a grateful glance when he cautiously raised the sheet a little with his head to see how his sister was taking the new arrangement.
>
> (Kafka 1992: 100–101)

All these events are described in plain language, light on adjectives, and almost devoid of metaphors. In this nightmarish scenario, flights of poetic imagery would detract from the starkness of the situation. The detached, almost clinical language also makes the incredible seem horrifyingly plausible. The effect is also to alienate the reader from 'normal' human behaviour. Before his transformation, Gregor had been supporting the family. The events that follow his misfortune reveal how selfish they really were. Despite their self-pity, they at least take steps to support themselves, including letting rooms. Through a crack in the door, Gregor watches his father greet the lodgers at their meal:

> The lodgers rose as one man and mumbled something into their beards. When they were alone again, they ate in almost complete silence. It seemed strange to Gregor that amongst all the various noises of the meal he could constantly pick out the sound of their

champing teeth, as if to demonstrate to Gregor that for eating teeth were needed, and even with the finest toothless jaws one could accomplish nothing.

(Kafka 1992: 115)

Needless to say, when the guests discover his presence, they seek another lodging. This is the event which precipitates Gregor's final crisis.

Other writers have experimented with non-human protagonists or with animals able to think and to speak. 'Dazzle', by the American Scott Bradfield, is written from the viewpoint of a dog who is 'particularly fond of pastry, philosophies of language and Third World political theory' (Bradfield 1993: 120), but wisely keeps his opinions hidden from his owners. 'The Parakeet and the Cat', also by Bradfield, uses extensive passages of dialogue between the smart bird and the manipulative but ultimately gullible cat. Another American, Joyce Carol Oates, invents a hybrid creature, both utterly goat-like and essentially girlish, in 'Secret Observations on the Goat-Girl' (Park and Heaton 1992). In 'The Débutante' by surrealist writer Leonora Carrington, a young woman hates balls so much her place is taken by a hyena she finds at the zoo (Carter 1986). These two women writers are using animal fables to ask what it really means to be that strange creature, a female.

Both Kate Atkinson's 'Temporal Anomaly' and Stephen King's 'That Feeling, You Can Only Say What it is in French', tell a story from the perspective of someone who is dead. Like 'Dazzle', 'Temporal Anomaly' extracts humour from the incongruity of the situation. Marianne is on her mobile phone, asking her mother for a recipe, when suddenly darkness sweeps over the car she is driving, making lemon meringue pie utterly irrelevant: 'And then Hades leant out of his chariot and punched a hole in the windscreen of her Audi and Marianne thought, "This is really going to hurt" ' (Atkinson 2003a: 272).

The dead Marianne lingers round her old home, watching daytime television while her husband and son put their lives back together. Like Kafka, Atkinson alienates her protagonist from her family by a radical transformation; their reaction to her death exposes the tensions underlying the relationships.

All of these stories share the mismatch between the mundane and the fantastic exploited by Kafka in 'Metamorphosis'. The reader suspends their disbelief in just one vital respect. Everything else stays the same. Gregor has turned into a beetle but he is also in trouble with his boss.

Dazzle is an intellectual, but he also stays true to his doggy nature, chasing after bitches and peeing on lamp-posts. The appeal of such stories lies in the interplay between these two equally vivid realities.

Another way to bring together the everyday and the extraordinary is to take the reader inside a character's fantasy world. In 'A Real Doll' (Cassini and Testa 2003), A. M. Homes's teenage narrator is fixated on his sister's Barbie doll: 'I'm dating Barbie. Three afternoons a week, while my sister is at dance class, I take Barbie away from Ken. I'm practicing for the future' (Cassini and Testa 2003: 145). Barbie speaks to him, just as toys often speak in a child's imagination. But the games he has in mind are rather unusual. In this darkly comic story, Homes highlights the perversity both of little girls and adolescent boys. Even though she loves Barbie, sister Jennifer nibbles away at her feet, scribbles on her and even switches her head with Ken's. Meanwhile the narrator abuses the doll sexually, his complex fantasies growing increasingly violent. In 'May', by the Scottish writer Ali Smith, a character falls in love with a tree, going so far as to pull up the floorboards in the hope of moving it into the house.

Stories such as 'Metamorphosis' subvert our assumptions about the everyday world, for instance that a family will stand by its members through the worst calamity. They make us question the rules we take for granted. What does it matter if Gregor is late at the office? Why should he go on accepting his lot as a wage slave supporting the whole family? This subversive potential can be used for a political purpose. By introducing the fantastic, a writer can give power to the weak and punish the mighty. Himself a Spokane and Coeur d'Alene Indian, Sherman Alexie entertains the reader with a 'magic realist' approach whilst also challenging racist oppression. In 'Ghost Dance' (Chabon 2003), Custer's Seventh Cavalry rise from their graves when a racist cop casually slaughters two Native Americans. The zombie soldiers rage through Montana feasting on human flesh. Like Kafka, Alexie leaves the story's exact interpretation to the reader. Tampering with the rules of nature, he unleashes powerful psychological symbols that he himself may not fully understand. Like the image-based writing I discussed in Chapter 2, fantastic writing calls upon the storyteller to tap into their unconscious mind. This will become even clearer in the next section, when we consider making use of myths.

Myth: 'The Company of Wolves' (Angela Carter, 1979)

In 'Temporal Anomaly', Kate Atkinson makes several references to other, well-known stories. One is the long-running television series *Buffy, the Vampire Slayer*. Another is the Greek myth of Persephone, who was abducted by the god of death. By using symbols, images and narratives from familiar sources, you can add extra layers of meaning to your story. Both Helen Simpson and Alice Munro integrate the Orpheus legend into contemporary stories. In Simpson's 'Opera', a neglected wife is on a corporate outing to Gluck's *Orfeo*. Surrounded by boorish businessmen, she is moved to tears by the music of loss and abandonment. In Munro's 'The Children Stay' (*The Love of a Good Woman*, 1998), the protagonist runs off with a young man she meets during an amateur production of Anouilh's play based on the myth. The intertextual relationship between the story and the Greek myth sheds light on the character's dilemma. Orpheus is allowed to rescue his dead wife from the Underworld on condition that he doesn't look back before they reach home. She pleads with him to look at her, and she vanishes forever. In this instance, the myth stands for the impossibility of going back on your decision. In another story, it would stand for something else. Myths are inexhaustible.

Folk tales are an especially potent source of material because they belong to the oldest and most widespread tradition, passed down through generations. They are remembered because they confront our most basic fears and desires. Italo Calvino, the Italian author of *Under the Jaguar Sun, Marcovaldo* and several other collections of marvellous and mythical tales, said 'Myth is the hidden part of every story, the buried part, the region that is still unexplored because there are as yet no words to enable us to get there' (Calvino 1997: 18). 'Little Red Riding Hood', 'Cinderella', 'Sleeping Beauty', 'Puss in Boots' and 'Bluebeard' were first committed to paper by a Frenchman, Perrault, in the seventeenth century, but versions of these tales have also surfaced in Germany, Japan and Korea. In one Italian version of 'Little Red Riding Hood' collected by Calvino, the little girl packs cakes for her journey, which she kindly gives to the river. Fleeing from the ogress who has taken her grandmother's place, the little girl is rewarded for generosity when the river sweeps the false grandmother away.

When Angela Carter turned to Perrault's version for 'The Company of Wolves', she merged the 'Little Red Riding Hood' story with the primeval legend of the werewolf. Many countries across the globe have superstitions about men who change into wolves. In Argentina, the seventh son was believed to roam the mountains as the fierce 'lobisón'. The superstition was so widespread, resulting in abortion and infanticide, that seventh sons were granted protection as presidential godsons. In Brazil, the transformation is less permanent, lasting only for the two hours after midnight.

The werewolf represents an untameable side to our nature, something dangerous lurking behind our civilized exterior. Like all mythical monsters, it is at once terrifying and fascinating. Carter revels in sensuous description, taking her time in the opening paragraphs to evoke the terrors of the natural world:

> You are always in danger in the forest, where no people are. Step between the portals of the great pines where the shaggy branches tangle about you, trapping the unwary traveller in nets as if the vegetation itself were in a plot with the wolves who live there, as though the wicked trees go fishing on behalf of their friends – step between the gateposts of the forest with the greatest trepidation and infinite precautions, for if you stray from the path for one instant, the wolves will eat you. They are grey as famine, they are as unkind as the plague.
>
> (Carter 1981: 111)

Carter transports us to a timeless peasant world where human beings are at the mercy of the elements. Nowadays, in the affluent West, only the most destitute have reason to dread the long winter. Yet we still react to the seasons, our moods lightening when spring comes along. Most of all, we fear the darkness. When M. R. James described 'the touch on the shoulder that comes when you are walking quickly homeward in the dark hours' (James 1993: 645–6), he was acknowledging atavistic fears dating back to early childhood. Carter has much in common with horror writers such as James, summoning 'the teeming perils of the night and the forest' (Carter 1981: 111) for her own purposes. In the darkness, we can see all kinds of mysterious shapes. Carter's 'teeming perils' begin with the actual danger of being attacked by hungry beasts, expanding to include supernatural threats – witches, ghosts, hobgoblins – culminating in the werewolf.

Unlike most horror yarns, 'The Company of Wolves' is very loosely structured. Although the language is quite complex, with a sophisticated vocabulary and literary allusions, it resembles a series of old wives' tales, addressed directly to the reader. We hear about a slaughtered wolf who turned back into a man and about a bridegroom who vanished on his wedding night. As in the South American legends, the number seven is significant: 'Seven years is a werewolf's natural span but if you burn his human clothing you condemn him to wolfishness for the rest of his life' (Carter 1981: 113).

About a third of the way through, these tales settle down into the 'Little Red Riding Hood' story. Carter's account is strong on visual detail, slipping between the past and present tense. Rather than taking the reader inside the character's head, she spreads the scene before you like a picture book. The girl is just a girl – any girl:

> Her breasts have just begun to swell; her hair is like lint, so fair it hardly makes a shadow on her pale forehead; her cheeks are an emblematic scarlet and white and she has just started her woman's bleeding, the clock inside her that will strike, henceforward, once a month.
>
> (Carter 1981: 113)

Carter is using fairy-tale imagery to explore the mixture of fear and excitement we feel at our first sexual awakening. When the unnamed girl sets off to visit Grandma, she is accosted by a handsome young hunter who shows her a clever invention:

> He said, if he plunged off the path into the forest that surrounded them, he could guarantee to arrive at her grandmother's house a good quarter of an hour before she did, plotting his way through the undergrowth with his compass, while she trudged the long way, along the winding path.
>
> (Carter 1981: 114–15)

She has been warned to conform, to plod the well-trodden path, while he takes the initiative. Accepting his wager, she promises a kiss if he reaches Grandma's ahead of her. Fulfilling our expectations, he duly surprises Grandma. When his true nature is revealed, beneath the human costume, the story's blatant eroticism is also undisguised:

> He strips off his shirt. His skin is the colour and texture of vellum. A crisp stripe of hair runs down his belly, his nipples are ripe and

dark as poison fruit but he's so thin you could count the ribs under his skin if only he gave you the time. He strips off his trousers and she can see how hairy his legs are. His genitals, huge. Ah! huge.

The last thing the old lady saw in all this world was a young man, eyes like cinders, naked as a stone, approaching her bed.

(Carter 1981: 116)

The werewolf is not only 'carnivore incarnate' (Carter 1981: 116); he is a naked man. And encountering a naked man can be quite a shock, especially if he is in a state of excitement. When the girl finally arrives, the narrative, once again, adheres to convention, repeating the familiar dialogue with the wolf disguised as Grandma:

What big eyes you have.
All the better to see you with.

(Carter 1981: 117)

But Carter extends the ritual into an erotic game; the girl clearly suspects what befell Grandma and is about to happen to her:

What shall I do with my blouse?
Into the fire with it, too, my pet.

(Carter 1981: 117)

Far more knowing than she lets on, the girl enjoys being in the wolf's power, while at the same time sensing male vulnerability in the howls of his companions beyond the lattice window.

As a feminist writer, Carter is tackling the ambiguities of sexual desire straying into some very uncomfortable areas. Fantasy allows the writer to represent extreme experiences without having to cope with the real-life repercussions. A real-life encounter with a dangerous man is quite another matter to the 'Bluebeard' story retold by Carter as 'The Bloody Chamber'. In the imagination we do all kinds of things we would never contemplate in reality.

Writing a fairy-tale fantasy gives free rein to unconscious imagery and to your powers of description. This does not mean abandoning any thought of conscious intention. For many writers, Carter included, intuition and control are finely balanced. Carter said that when she started a story she set herself a number of questions, but that these were questions without a right answer. The British writer A. S. Byatt often uses mythical and fairy-tale elements in her work. The idea for 'A Stone Woman' came to her during a stay in hospital when the nerve-endings in her stomach became numb. She began to wonder what it would feel like if you were turned to stone. But she has said that once the writing was underway the words themselves took over. She lost sight of the original impulse behind the story.

In the essays collected as *Six Memos For the Next Millennium*, Calvino analyses the imaginative process and the nature of storytelling, especially in relation to myth. He says that for him a story always originates as a purely visual image – 'an image that for some reason strikes me as charged with meaning, even if I cannot formulate this meaning in discursive or conceptual terms' (Calvino 1996: 89). This is the case even when the stimulus is verbal – a scientific expression, for instance. Other images start to gather around this first image and, as he starts to mentally organize these images and then to put words on paper, the search for meaning gets underway.

As these images fall into place, patterns emerge. The visual details in 'The Company of Wolves' are enjoyable for their sheer richness and intensity, but they have also been chosen for their explicit symbolism; for instance, the bright red of the girl's shawl and her cheeks stand for menstrual blood and the blood that is shed when she loses her virginity. In practice, an author's intentions are deeply intertwined with the unconscious processes at work in the writing. There is no point in trying to untangle the two. As Carter once said, 'I write the way I write, because that's the way I write' (Haffenden 1986: 93). In some of the activities at the end of the chapter you will be experimenting with symbolic imagery, which you can use in every type of fiction. As you will discover for yourself, developing new thoughts and ideas through the act of writing is one of the most exciting aspects of becoming a storyteller.

Parallel worlds: 'Tlön, Uqbar, Orbis Tertius' (Jorge Luis Borges, 1962)

Like Angela Carter, Jorge Luis Borges immerses the reader in an imaginary world, packed with precise details. But Borges goes even further. While Carter uses her timeless setting as a backdrop, Borges designs an entire alternative universe. If you have ever taken part in a role-playing game, you will appreciate the intricacy of this undertaking.

'Tlön, Uqbar, Orbis Tertius' masquerades as a scholarly essay, backed up with references to obscure publications and arcane 'facts'. From 'Metamorphosis' onwards, we have seen how important it is to make your fantasy seem plausible by rooting it in the real world. The details in Borges's story sound very convincing, especially since they are conveyed in the detached and even pedantic language that you would expect from a reputable source:

> I owe the discovery of Uqbar to the conjunction of a mirror and an encyclopedia. The mirror troubled the depths of a corridor in a country house on Gaona Street in Ramos Mejía; the encyclopedia is fallaciously called *The Anglo-American Cyclopaedia* (New York, 1917) and is a literal but delinquent reprint of the *Enyclopaedia Britannica* of 1902.
>
> (Borges 1971: 27)

Over dinner at the country house with his friend Bioy, the narrator is told that 'one of the heresiarchs of Uqbar had declared that mirrors and copulation are abominable, because they increase the number of men' (Borges 1971: 27). No such place is found in the encyclopaedia or in the atlas. The narrator concludes that his host made it up. But the next day Bioy proves his story with some extra pages in Volume XLVI of the encyclopaedia: '*For one of those gnostics, the visible universe was an illusion or (more precisely) a sophism. Mirrors and fatherhood are abominable because they multiply and disseminate that universe*' (Borges 1971: 28).

As he analyses this text and pursues others, the narrator piles reference on reference, leading us ever more deeply into the fictional labyrinth. Real and invented places and names are mixed up together; Bioy was an actual friend of Borges. De Quincey was a real writer, but did he actually mention a 'Johannes Valentinus Andreä' in *Writings*, Volume XIII, as the story claims? Does such a book exist? Some readers respond to the story as a brain-teaser, enjoying the mental exercise, just as some readers like solving fictional crimes. For others, it doesn't really matter if you don't quite understand 'heresiarch' or 'sophism', or if you lose track of the long trail of references. Few of us have the philosophical training to fully comprehend the ideas in Borges's stories, but their intellectual complexity does mean you can return to them again and again, each time grasping a little bit more. Borges breaks the usual guidelines on sticking to just a few characters and incidents in a short story. His works prove that, far from being a limiting form, short fiction can be ambitious in its scope.

Despite their labours, Bioy and the narrator fail to find any documentary evidence beyond a tentative link between Uqbar and mythical realms known as 'Mlejnas' and 'Tlön'. Then, by chance, the eleventh volume of *A First Encyclopaedia of Tlön* falls into the narrator's hands – in circumstances far too complicated for me to explain in these few pages. Now at last the narrator discovers Uqbar's true status:

> Two years before I had discovered, in a volume of a certain pirated encyclopaedia, a superficial description of a non-existent country; now chance afforded me something more precious and arduous. Now I held in my hands a vast methodical fragment of an unknown planet's entire history, with its architecture and its playing cards, with the dread of its mythologies and the murmur of its languages, with its emperors and its seas, with its minerals and its birds and its fish, with its algebra and its fire, with its theological and metaphysical controversy. And all of it articulated, coherent, with no visible doctrinal intent or tone of parody.
>
> (Borges 1971: 31)

This declaration serves as a manifesto for writing other worlds. Some writers invent utopias – perfect worlds we might aspire to – or dystopias, showing how society might deteriorate still further if current trends persist. But this particular cosmos exists in its own right, not as a political instrument. It is 'articulated, coherent', an intricate device designed for our amazement, and completed, so far as is possible, down to the tiniest detail: 'the intimate laws which govern it have been formulated, at least provisionally' (Borges 1971: 32).

But of course this manufactured world can't be completed, any more than you could itemize every aspect of life on Planet Earth. Pieced together over the centuries by a loose network of scientists, artists and thinkers, Tlön is not a world of solid objects but of process and appearance. In some of its dialects, the language doesn't even have nouns. Sometimes meanings are conveyed mostly by verbs, in other regions by adjectives: 'They do not say "moon" but rather "round airy-light on dark" or "pale-orange-of-the-sky" or any other such combination' (Borges 1971: 33). Tlön's special quality is that it cannot be fixed. It can only be imagined, and this is why its reality fluctuates according to mental projections: 'In the most ancient regions of Tlön, the duplication of lost objects is not infrequent. Two persons look for a pencil; the first finds it and says nothing; the second finds a second pencil, no less real, but closer to his expectations' (Borges 1971: 37–8).

If you have ever lost your keys, then suddenly found them, right where they ought to have been in the first place, you will sympathize with ideas about shifting dimensions and a parallel universe.

The narrator ends his story by lamenting the newspaper exposure which, after centuries, has finally caught up with the secret Freemasonry of *Orbis Tertius*:

> Manuals, anthologies, summaries, literal versions, authorized re-editions and pirated editions of the Greatest Work of Man flooded and still flood the earth. Almost immediately reality yielded on more than one account. The truth is that it longed to yield. Ten years ago any symmetry with a semblance of order – dialectical materialism, anti-Semitism, Nazism – was sufficient to entrance the minds of men. How could one do other than submit to Tlön, to the minute and vast evidence of an orderly planet?
>
> (Borges 1971: 42)

In fact, Borges is arguing against the perception that reality is 'orderly'. He is opposing totalitarian ideas, which claim to know the answer to everything. He is saying that such systems are themselves fictions. Once again, the fantastic challenges our assumptions about the 'real' world.

In his essay 'The Argentine Writer and Tradition', Borges explained that he had tried for years to capture the essence of Buenos Aires, the city where he was born. It was only when he turned his back on realism, 'abandoning myself to a dream' that he found himself accidentally catching its spirit (Borges 1971: 216). Using the fantastic relieves you from the responsibility of staying absolutely faithful to the literal truth. By drawing on fantasy images, you may find yourself probing a deeper truth than can be expressed through surface reality. The activities at the end of the chapter invite you to introduce symbolism, myth and the mysterious into your work as a way of making your writing more complex and multilayered.

Both Borges and Carter were avid readers who absorbed other writings in their own work. Carter was especially influenced by Isak Dinesen, the Danish author of *Seven Gothic Tales*, when she was writing *The Bloody*

Chamber. Borges was fond of the old-fashioned yarns written by Stevenson, Kipling and Poe. He said he much preferred the concision of short stories to the shapelessness of novels. In old age when he was blind, these stories were read aloud to him often. He must have known them very well, savouring each line. Whatever type of story you intend to write yourself, the best way to learn your craft is through extensive reading. All of the writers included in this chapter have been playful, curious and provocative. These are the qualities you should look for in your writing as you surrender yourself to the 'voluntary dream'.

Activity 1   Metamorphosis

Like many of the activities throughout the book, the exercises in this section are designed largely to jump-start your imagination. Experimenting with the mythical, the magical and the fantastic should encourage you to take risks in your work, even if you are primarily a realist or an autobiographical writer. For the first four exercises, you should write quickly and intuitively, producing drafts which can be polished later.

For this first activity, imagine you have an extraordinary ability, inexplicable in normal human terms. An example might be invisibility or the ability to fly. Amongst the activities at the end of Chapter 2 there was an exercise on an especially acute sense of smell or hearing. Remember, in all other respects you are an average person, leading a humdrum existence. You are definitely *not* a superhero. Using the first person, describe how you discover this ability. Do you keep it a secret? How does it change your life?

This exercise follows the strategy used by 'Metamorphosis' and other stories in the 'Altering Reality' section by introducing just one extraordinary element into an ordinary world. To make the metamorphosis plausible you must also be able to suggest mundane reality. I have not specified word limits for the activities in this chapter. You should now be able to gauge the potential of each idea for short sketches or drafts of longer stories.

Activity 2   Life but not as we know it

Using the third person, describe the world as seen by someone or something who is not human. By 'not human' I mean an animal – including fish, insects, birds or reptiles; a god or a mythical being; or even, stretching the definition, a ghost or a spirit. (If you are intending to be a deity, look first at Activity 4.) Anticipating the next chapter, you could make them an alien life form, but only if they are visiting Earth.

This activity is partially an exercise in viewpoint, moving on from the previous first-person narrative. In all storytelling, it is vital to establish a clear point of view. When you have finished, look again at my reading of Kafka's 'Metamorphosis'. While writing in the third person, Kafka filters most of the narrative through Gregor, enduring with him all the excruciating physical adjustments he is forced to make. The term 'focalization', taken from the French critic Genette, helps clarify this idea of viewpoint or perspective. I used the expression 'camera's eye' when I discussed the episode of Gregor's father forcing him back inside his room; the author depicts the scene through the 'lens' of the character. Another good example of 'focalization' is Mansfield's use of Bertha's perspective in 'Bliss' (see Chapter 2). Inexperienced writers often have problems with viewpoint. Here's an example: 'With my face framed by a blazing fire and the sound of stampeding soldiers circling round, I never felt so trapped'. An onlooker would see that visual image of the character's face from the outside, but that is not how the narrator would perceive himself at that moment, from the inside.

Of course, 'focalization' includes more than what the character actually sees. It relates to all the senses and to mental processes – the character's whole 'take' on the world. In 'To Build a Fire', an adventure story by the American Jack London, the focalization alternates between a gold prospector and his husky dog, who is much more attuned to the harsh environment of the Yukon. London contrasts the dog's sensitivity to exact degrees of cold with the limited perceptions of even a fairly experienced human traveller. In the description, consider how your character interacts with its environment. If it is a ghost or a spirit, does it have any physical sensations? If it is a divinity, does it ever make contact with human beings?

As a way of structuring the material into a narrative, introduce conflict. Put your character's way of life under threat. An animal character may be struggling to survive like London's husky or the bird in Scott Bradfield's 'The Parakeet and the Cat'. Spirits can be exorcized, or a haunted building earmarked for demolition.

Activity 3   Intertextuality

Most of us write intertextually without ever thinking about it. All it means is that stories feed into one another. The many folk versions of the tale we know as 'Cinderella' have influenced each other. Its basic 'rags-to-riches' plot is echoed in many different forms in every medium. New writers are sometimes fixated on originality and are disheartened to discover an idea has been 'done'. But true originality lies in style and structure; it is how you handle the material that really matters. Referring to a well-known story within your own fiction expands the possibilities; it is like opening a door out of your story into another.

Part of Angela Carter's interest in folk tales stemmed from a desire to return to the mood of the original stories. She felt that the earthy and violent stories from the oral tradition had been censored when they were printed for middle-class readers. The Caribbean writer Andrew Salkey also reclaimed the oral tradition, by reworking stories about Anancy the spider. In producing these stories he was announcing that writers belonged to their own literary culture, independent from the white colonial inheritance. Feminist writers have also subverted the conventions of the fairy tales in examples such as Suniti Namjoshi's *Feminist Fables* and A. S. Byatt's 'The Story of the Eldest Princess' (Park and Heaton 1992). Margaret Atwood's 'Bluebeard's Egg' refers to the story within a contemporary tale about a marriage breaking down.

For this exercise, rewrite a well-known story of your own choosing. Examples might include:

- **Fairy tales or folk tales.** As well as the European folk tales collected by Perrault, look into the *Tales from the Thousand and One Nights*. There are also local and national legends – in England, the stories surrounding Robin Hood or King Arthur. Rip Van Winkle, a character created by Washington Irving, has become a part of American folklore. Another source to consider is the folk ballad. 'The Raggle-Taggle Gypsies' is just one of many traditional English folk songs. Its many different versions tell the story of a married woman who takes to the open road, turning her back on a pampered lifestyle – a tale of 'riches to rags'.
- **Myths.** I have already mentioned the tale of Midas as an example of tragic irony (see Chapter 3). Alice Munro and Helen Simpson both

used the story of Orpheus and Eurydice; Kate Atkinson also refers to the Underworld, this time through the figure of Persephone ('Temporal Anomaly'). Ted Chiang's 'Tower of Babylon' visualizes the biblical legend of the Tower of Babel, so tall it reached to Heaven.

• **Literary sources.** Take an instantly recognizable fictional character and write a new story round them, perhaps putting them into an entirely different setting. The nineteenth-century English writers Charles and Mary Lamb made Shakespeare's plays accessible for children by turning them into short stories. Sherlock Holmes has been a particular favourite for literary reworkings – most recently in the horror anthology *Shadows Over Baker Street*.

• **Living legends.** In Robert Olen Butler's 'JFK Secretly Attends Jackie Auction', it is revealed that the late President John F. Kennedy was not really killed by the assassin's bullet. Instead he has been affected by a peculiar type of brain damage. He is unable to keep state secrets. After many years in hiding, he attends the auction of his widow Jackie's effects, held after her death. 'The Assassination of John Fitzgerald Kennedy Considered as a Downhill Motor Race' by the British writer J. G. Ballard is exactly what the title says it is. The effect of using an iconic figure such as JFK is quite startling. This strategy overlaps with the concept of 'alternative history', discussed in the next chapter. But here the emphasis is more on subverting a media megastar than thinking about historical cause and effect.

In your reworking, choose from any combination of the following strategies:

1 Update the story.
2 Tell it from the perspective of a minor character, even someone who doesn't figure in the original version. The English writer Julian Barnes's 'The Stowaway' is narrated by one of the less likely creatures on Noah's Ark.
3 Change the ending or other key elements in the plot, such as Kennedy's death in Robert Olen Butler's story.
4 Change the genre – for example, rewrite 'Snow White' as a Sherlock Holmes mystery. Ballard's story was itself inspired by 'The Crucifixion Considered as an Uphill Bicycle Race' by the French surrealist Alfred Jarry. Are there any historical events you could recast in sporting terms?

5   Give us the prequel or the sequel. What happened after the Prince won his Princess? How did the Wicked Witch make her career choice?

6   Use just one element as a symbol within an original story. Myths are especially good at providing ready-made symbols because they are so familiar. One example is the apple given to Eve by the serpent in the biblical Garden of Eden. Another is the gigantic wooden horse given to the Trojans by their enemies, the Greeks. Once it was inside the city wall, hordes of warriors poured out of a secret compartment. The Trojan Horse has become a byword for something dangerous which appears innocent. There are countless other examples. You could even use the symbol as a title. Taken from an African American spiritual, Katherine Anne Porter's 'Pale Horse, Pale Rider' refers to one of the Horsemen of the Apocalypse mentioned in the biblical Book of Revelations. It is an all-too-appropriate title for a story set during the lethal flu epidemic of the First World War.

You can write your story as a fully fledged fantasy like 'The Company of Wolves'; or you can use elements of the tale to construct another type of story, which may not even be recognizably based on the original.

Activity 4   Playing God

Write a first-person account of life on earth today, told from the point of view of a fictional deity or supreme being. This entity has the power to intervene in human existence. To him, her or it, we are no more than puppets or chess pieces. She, he or it may intervene for moral reasons, to punish the wicked and reward the virtuous, out of mischief, or for any other reason you can devise. Show the consequences.

   Your fictional being is omnipotent and probably omniscient; he/she/it can do anything and knows everything. You are using a first-person narrator who is also a character in the story. Events are also focalized through this consciousness. 'Omniscient narrator' is a technical term for an anonymous, impersonal storyteller in a third-person narrative. It is the 'once upon a time' narrator; Angela Carter uses an omniscient narrator in 'The Company of Wolves'. This type of storyteller is a puppet-master, like the deity you have just invented. You will be making use of an omniscient narrator in the next exercise; there is another example in Maupassant's 'Country Living' (see Chapter 6).

Activity 5   The island, Part I

Create an imaginary island. You can place this island anywhere or nowhere. Its landscape and people are up to you. It could be densely populated with a thriving capital city, or it could have just a scattering of inhabitants. But it is entirely fictional. Within this fictional space you can invent whatever you like. Writing as quickly as you can, spend ten minutes describing the island. Use note form if you find this easier. There may be one or two gaps in your ideas, which will be filled gradually through the process of writing and thinking.

Every year on the island a special ceremony or ritual takes place. It could be linked to a familiar festival, such as New Year or harvest, but it is significantly different to anything in the real world. Make some notes on the ritual.

As you may have gathered, this is an exercise in creating an alternative reality, although on a smaller scale than Borges's Tlön and Uqbar. Turn your notes on the island and the ritual into a third-person account, told by an omniscient narrator.

It is possible to adapt this type of exercise for a workshop, with group discussions making the decisions about the island and its customs. You can even draw maps and diagrams if you so wish.

Activity 6   The island, Part II

Continuing the previous exercise, you are going to rewrite your account of the island from the point of view of a stranger newly arrived there. This first-person narrative takes the form of a journal, letter or e-mail. You will need to decide what the stranger is doing on the island, how they got there and of course who they are; one of the most important factors is their opinion of the ritual. Do they approve or disapprove? Do they get involved? Do they misunderstand?

Now you will 'frame' this narrative within another. The framing narrative is told by someone reading what your first narrator has written. They will describe how they received or found the stranger's account. This could have occurred soon after it was written or some time later. The second narrator will also tell us what they know about what happened after the account was written, including the fate of the stranger. There may still be some mystery surrounding this whole story and even the existence of the island itself.

This 'story within a story' could even be multiplied further, like those Russian dolls that fit one inside another. It is an example of the multiple narratives used by Borges. The traditional yarn often embeds a story within a story. In Conan Doyle's 'The Red-Headed League', passages of dialogue take over the narrative, notably Jabez Wilson's account of his unusual employment (see Chapter 1).

Activity 7   Blue

Spend ten minutes writing down as many things as you can think of associated with the colour blue. These can be as general or as personal as you like. The chances are that you have come up with a wide range of images, some of them contradictory. The calm blue of the ocean contrasts with the blues you get when you're feeling lonely – or is there perhaps something connecting these two moods? You may have pictured someone's blue eyes, or seen a pair of blue jeans. Select just one of those images as the starting point for a story. The exercise is inspired by Carter's use of red in 'The Company of Wolves'. As you write, explore the further ideas and images associated with the colour. You can introduce your other 'blue' images, but you shouldn't feel you have to weave all of them in.

Afterwards, look at Michael Joyce's 'Twelve Blue. Story in Eight Bars' as an example of how images and symbols can be used to develop non-linear narrative in hyperspace (Joyce 2003).

5

What if?

Science fiction, the fantastic, the yarn and the fable are all interrelated. 'Tlön, Uqbar, Orbis Tertius' could be classed as science fiction, and so could several of the other stories I mentioned in both the previous chapter and Chapter 1. Some prefer the term 'speculative fiction', downplaying the emphasis on scientific hardware and the geek image that used to be so off-putting – especially for women, who are now much more visible amongst the SF community. Whatever the initials stand for, 'SF' covers a very broad tradition, given a new lease of life at the turn of the millennium. Historically, the classification has covered everything from the 'hard' technological fiction of Isaac Asimov's robot stories to the mythological fantasies of Ursula K. Le Guin, H. P. Lovecraft's weird tales and David Brin's update on genetic engineering; from the thought experiments of Philip K. Dick to the heroic adventures of Robert E. Howard's Conan the Barbarian. Like the fantastic, science fiction is a great opportunity for you to extend your imaginative range through a variety of styles and techniques.

Science fiction is especially suited to the short story, because it so often turns on a single idea. It also has an active and committed readership, supporting an enormous number of magazines and specialized presses. In the USA, *Amazing Stories* and *Astounding* (later *Analog*) have been running almost continually since the 1920s. The British *Interzone*, founded in 1982, has built an international reputation by publishing new talent alongside established names. As you might expect, SF is well served by the Internet. Most of the magazines have associated web sites. A web site like Infinity Plus can provide a huge amount of online fiction, resources and links to other sites. All of these outlets need material, and science-fiction readers naturally evolve into science-fiction writers. In a lonely business, science fiction offers writers a genuine sense of community.

Don't be daunted if you are not scientifically educated. Some well-known writers, including Isaac Asimov and David Brin, have been trained scientists; but William Gibson coined the concepts of cyberspace and virtual reality without even owning a computer. As the contemporary American writer Thomas M. Disch says, 'If writers had the intellectual wherewithal to handle quantum mechanics, they'd be physicists, not fiction writers' (McCaffery 1990: 116). But if you are seriously interested in the SF market, you do need to immerse yourself in that broad tradition. The twentieth-century American author Philip K. Dick describes himself at the age of twelve, chancing upon a magazine called *Stirring Science Stories* on the shelves next to the comic books and reading it all the way home. In those pages he found the thing he would one day explore as a writer, 'a medium in which the full play of the human imagination can operate, ordered, of course, by reason and consistent development' (Dick 1995: 9).

Dick says that in order to sit down and write he has to have an idea. In this respect, SF differs slightly from the type of image-based fiction I discussed in Chapter 2, which can emerge more gradually from sketches and impressions. This does not mean that the writing will never diverge from your original idea, but in order to make a start you need to ask yourself, 'what if . . .?' What if bacteria could communicate? What if human beings could remember the future? The answer to the first question – or, at least, a possible answer – lies in the introduction to a non-existent book, *Eruntics*, published alongside several other fake introductions in *Imaginary Magnitude* by the Polish writer Stanislaw Lem. The second is addressed in 'Story of Your Life' by the American Ted Chiang. The British writer Brian Aldiss uses another question, 'Who Can Replace a Man?', as the title of his story exploring a future where manual work is carried out by robots (Shippey 2003). Aldiss imagines what would happen if suddenly there were no humans left to set the controls. Isaac Asimov wrote 'Nightfall' after John W. Campbell, the editor of *Astounding*, drew his attention to a quotation from the great American thinker Ralph Waldo Emerson: 'If the stars were to appear but one night in a thousand years, how would men believe and adore and preserve for many generations the remembrance of the city of God which they had seen'. Campbell thought they would go mad; why not write a story about it?

All of these examples are based on what is sometimes called a 'novum'. The critic Darko Suvin coined this term as a shorthand for any new element that marks out a difference from current reality. The novum could be an amazing new invention or an extraordinary event, such as a visit from outer space. And, of course, any novum will generate further complications. The central idea in George R. R. Martin's 'The Way of Cross and Dragon' (Shippey 2003) is that the One True Interstellar Catholic Church of Earth and the Thousand Worlds exerts inter-planetary authority, rooting out any local heresies. The notion that a religion considered by some to be outdated might persist, in mutated form, far into the future, is itself extremely daring. We often assume that societies far ahead in space or time will be more rational and streamlined than our own. Martin has thought differently.

An interstellar church requires extraterrestrial beings. Martin's narra-tor, a Knight Inquisitor, is commanded by an aquatic bishop, whose rancid smell is off-putting to humans: 'his arms moved as he spoke, four ponderous clubs of mottled green-grey flesh churning the water, and the dirty white cilia around his breathing hole trembled with each word' (Shippey 2003: 456). The heretics on the planet Arion worship St Judas Iscariot, contradicting the Gospel accounts of Christ's death and resurrection. When the Knight Inquisitor confronts this heresy, he dis-covers that its legends are deliberate fabrications, devised by a secret order. The Liars know that life is meaningless, yet realize that religious faith increases happiness. They therefore set about improving religious myths, strengthening belief. Martin's story operates like a set of boxes, each within the other. Their intellectual content has to be put in a con-vincing context, so Martin provides new solar systems, extraterrestrial beings and the starship *Truth of Christ*.

Science fiction needs a novum. But the story's interest lies in the way the characters react to the problems generated by the new element. The plot develops as the writer of 'The Way of Cross and Dragon' debates belief and doubt at a sophisticated level. The questions raised in mind of its narrator will also resonate in the reader's mind. No matter how much hardware it includes, science fiction brings us face to face with profoundly human dilemmas. As the contemporary British writer J. G. Ballard has said:

> It looks at the future and tries to put the emotion in as well, so it is not a cold, theoretical prediction of what the future is like. It is a visualized future in which human beings move about and react to these changed circumstances, and that is its function.
>
> (Bigsby 2000: 78)

The unknown: 'In the Abyss' (H. G. Wells, 1897)

One of the simplest plot structures is the journey into the unknown. When few Europeans had explored the other continents, travellers' tales detailed mythological tribes and fantastic animals in the New World. Nowadays we are more easily amazed by space travel than voyages across the globe. But similar principles apply. In outer space or on the home planet, the writer places numerous perils along the path. These may continue at the destination. But once you are there, you have the freedom to create astonishing new life forms, breathtaking landscapes – sometimes even entire civilizations.

The example I have chosen is from H. G. Wells, who produced many of the most enduring SF novels and stories around a hundred years ago, including *The Time Machine* and *The War of the Worlds*. His story 'In the Abyss' goes not to outer space, this time, but underwater, to the ocean's depths. Science-fiction writers tend to be more interested in ideas and experiences than in individual psychology, and human beings often function primarily as witnesses. Wells's explorer, Elstead, is given to us without any personal history or anything apart from his name to differentiate him from the other characters, Steevens and Weybridge. In some of his stories, Wells dispenses with names altogether; in 'The Land Ironclads', he sticks to 'the war correspondent', 'the young lieutenant', 'the artist' and so on. The characters' anonymity makes them seem universal, adding to the story's timeless quality.

In science fiction, a lot of new, sometimes mind-boggling, information needs to be put across to the reader without holding up the narrative. Like his contemporary Arthur Conan Doyle, Wells uses dialogue to outline the key facts at the start. Since Steevens is a new arrival on the ship, Weybridge is obliged to explain the design of Elstead's vessel, a steel sphere built to resist high pressure. The first few pages are packed with technical preparations, which serve both to impress the reader with scientific know-how and to signal all the dangers of travelling five miles beneath the surface.

When Wells was writing, underwater travel was at the cutting edge. Submarine technology has advanced since then, but the deepest parts of the oceans, such as the Atlantic Trench, still remain inaccessible. Later writers such as Arthur C. Clarke, Isaac Asimov and Ray Bradbury were imagining interplanetary travel during the space race when the moon landings were being planned, and it seemed only a matter of time before human beings would colonize the entire solar system. Science fiction was simply pushing the envelope further. Nowadays space travel is not quite so newsworthy but writers such as Stephen J. Gould, Richard Dawkins and Daniel Dennett have made other kinds of science accessible. You can find new explanations of evolution, theories of time or artificial intelligence in television documentaries, newspapers and magazines such as *New Scientist* and *Scientific American*. Knowledge is always moving on, each new advance revealing how much more there still is to be discovered. As I write, a European space probe is planning to investigate the weather on Venus. The wind there travels at 100 metres a second, and clouds of sulphuric acid hover above a surface that reaches 400 degrees centigrade. With luck the space probe will bring back the scientific data, but we can only begin to experience the reality through the imagination.

The extended dialogue at the start of Wells's story may remind you of Conan Doyle and 'The Red-Headed League'. 'In the Abyss' is a yarn, and Wells keeps to the conventions. He builds up suspense when Elstead is launched on his solo voyage, describing the long wait for his return. Just as Weybridge and Steevens are giving up hope, they glimpse the sphere in the distance. After much difficulty, they retrieve Elstead, unconscious and seemingly traumatized. Like many yarns, the narrative is pieced together through testimonies – through dialogue and through the account Elstead is said to have given when at last he recovers.

As I said earlier, in relation to 'The Way of Cross and Dragon', at its heart the science-fiction plot centres on its characters' problems. Elstead may not be a rounded character, but in many respects that makes his story more compelling. He is an everyman, and we concentrate on his vivid description without the distractions of thinking, for instance, about his life back home. At first we focus on the terrors of the journey as the sphere drops towards the ocean's floor:

It was just like the start of a lift, he said, only it kept on. One has to imagine what that means, that keeping on. It was then of all times that Elstead repented of his adventure. He saw the chances against him in an altogether new light. He thought of the big cuttle-fish people knew to exist in the middle waters, the kind of things they find half digested in whales at times, or floating dead and rotten and half-eaten by fish. Suppose one caught hold and wouldn't let go. And had the clockwork really been sufficiently tested?

(Wells 2000: 145)

Exactly what you or I might feel if we were unlucky – or lucky? – enough to be in a similar situation. The start of a lift is something most of us can relate to, but the 'keeping on' multiplies the familiar sensation, helping us to imagine an entirely new experience. Soon Elstead's fears are overtaken by curiosity:

He peered out of the window. There were no more bubbles now, and the hissing had stopped. Outside there was a heavy blackness – as black as black velvet – except where the electric light pierced the empty water and showed the colour of it – a yellow-green. Then three things like shapes of fire swam into sight, following each other through the water. Whether they were little and near or big and far off he could not tell.

(Wells 2000: 145–6)

The language is very exact, adding credibility to Elstead's story. But what he actually sees remains imprecise; he is describing shapes and luminescence, and is unsure about their scale. Because 'we see the thing darkly in fragmentary glimpses', the sense of mystery and power is intensified, and the reader's imagination activated further. We aren't just passive spectators, like a cinema audience. We fill in the details. Prose fiction also has the advantage when Wells introduces humanoid life forms. No need for special effects; we can see for ourselves:

Two large and protruding eyes projected from eyes in chameleon fashion, and it had a broad reptilian mouth with horny lips beneath its little nostrils. In the position of the ears were two huge gill-covers, and out of these floated a branching tree of coralline filaments, almost like the treelike gills that every young ray and shark possess.

But the humanity of the face was not the most extraordinary thing about the creature. It was a biped; its almost globular body was poised on a tripod of two frog-like legs and a long thick tail, and its fore limbs, which grotesquely caricatured the human hand, much as a frog's do, carried a long shaft of bone, tipped with copper. The colour of the creature was variegated; its heads, hands, and legs were purple; but its skin, which hung loosely upon it, even as clothes might do, was a phosphorescent grey. And it stood there, blinded by the light.

(Wells 2000: 147)

Wells has observed creatures that live underwater and has applied his knowledge to alien life forms. He has thought about how these beings might adapt to their environment, equipping them with gills and with limbs that can manipulate, so that they are capable of building the sub-terranean cities we are about to discover. Arthur C. Clarke's 'Second Dawn' (Shippey 2003) is told from the viewpoint of a non-human race, living in a distant universe. The Atheleni are gifted with immense mental powers, including telepathy, but in practical terms are restricted by their physique. Unlike human beings, whose opposable thumbs enable them to manipulate objects, they are unable to make anything. They have no manual skills. Like Clarke's story, Ursula K. Le Guin's 'Semley's Necklace' (Shippey 2003) populates a planet with several distinct races, equipped with different skills. In each case, the alien culture is adjusted to the native environment.

Because Elstead is the only witness, and a traumatized one at that, his evidence is 'circumstantial', yet, according to the narrator, backed up by eminent scientists who 'see no reason why intelligent, water-breathing, vertebrated creatures, inured to low temperature and enormous pressure, and of such a heavy structure that neither alive nor dead would they float, might not live upon the bottom of the deep sea, and quite unsuspected by us, descendants like ourselves of the great Theriomorpha of the New Red Sandstone age' (Wells 2000: 149–50). Wells has thought of everything. You may wonder why in all these centuries no one has ever found a trace of the creatures; the reason is that they cannot float to the surface, not even as corpses, like the whales we sometimes find along a beach. The American science-fiction writer Robert Heinlein once said, any new theory must be, so to speak, watertight; 'it may be far-fetched, it may seem fantastic, but it must *not* be at variance with observed facts' (James 1994: 59). The rules of nature still apply within the fantasy you created, as discovered when completing the activities at the end of the previous chapter.

The sphere is captured by the creatures, is worshipped by them and finally released, apparently when its rope frays against their altar. In the closing paragraphs, we learn that Elstead has vanished, attempting to repeat his expedition: 'but it is hardly probable that no further attempt will be made to verify his strange story of these hitherto unsuspected cities of the deep sea' (Wells 2000: 151). The story is designed to astonish the reader, to increase our sense of wonder and to whet our appetite for discovery. Although it is very much concerned with ideas, Wells's fiction is thrilling. It is not dry or abstract; we are plunged into an intensely physical world.

Despite the technological advances which enable Elstead to make his trip, the journey reveals how little we really know about the universe, and how restricted we are by our physical capacities, for instance our inability to breathe underwater. This emphasis on looking at human nature from a wider perspective is one of the great advantages of writing science fiction, reminding us of our limitations and our frailty. Wells's own story 'The Star' and J. G. Ballard's 'Report from an Obscure Planet' both prophesy the extinction of the human race. Ballard has said that in its ability to warn us of the horrors of the future, science fiction may be the only literary form capable of direct influence over events (Bigsby 2000: 71–86). If you are concerned with ecology, the environment or weapons of mass destruction, science fiction could be the genre for you.

Utopias and dystopias

Wells is often hailed as a prophet. He foresaw mechanized forms of warfare in 'The Land Ironclads', and 'The Star' anticipates modern anxieties concerning global warming. But, for the moment at least, time travel is off the agenda; and while undersea explorers may plumb the ocean's depths, they are unlikely to do so by clockwork. No one can predict the future with 100 per cent accuracy, but science fiction can provide an inspiration or a warning, or a contrast with today. Feminist writers have often turned to science fiction for exactly this reason. In Joanna Russ's 'When It Changed' (Gilbert and Gubar 1985), men have long since been made extinct. This challenges assumptions that humanity has to be split between genders or that men are necessary. In 'The Screwfly Solution', Racoona Sheldon (Shippey 2003) applies biological methods of pest control to human beings. By using pheromones, another race can turn male against female, eradicating the species as surely as human beings destroy insects. The zeal with which the human males commit 'femicide' against their own women is made frighteningly plausible.

It is often said that science fiction is as much about the present as the future; making this point, Ballard says that his own stories, now up to fifty years old, are set in a 'visionary present' (Ballard 2002: ix). Writers maximize trends to the utmost to show where we might be heading. China already limits families to one child, while in most urban societies social rank is determined by access to a good education. In that light, selection by 'Revised Genetic Testing', explained in Disch's 'Problems of Creativeness' (Shippey 2003) seems like a logical progression. Individuals can only reproduce if they pass their exams.

Disch's pessimistic forecast constitutes a 'dystopia', an imaginary place which is uniformly depressing. Inspired by the growth of mass advertising in the consumer boom of the 1960s, Ballard's 'The Subliminal Man' describes traffic signs which transmit subliminal signals, inducing an unsuspecting public to buy unnecessary products. Driving home, Ballard's protagonist, Franklin, begins to suspect that something odd is going on:

> Two hundred yards away was a roadside auto-mart, and Franklin abruptly remembered that he needed some cigarettes. Swinging the car down the entrance ramp, he joined the queue passing the self-service dispenser at the far end of the rank. The auto-mart was packed with cars, each of the five purchasing ranks lined with tired-looking men hunched over their wheels.
>
> Inserting his coins (paper money was no longer in circulation, unmanageable by the automats) he took a carton from the dispenser. This was the only brand of cigarettes available – in fact there was only one brand of everything – though giant economy packs were an alternative. Moving off, he opened the dashboard locker.
>
> Inside, still sealed in their wrappers, were three other cartons.
>
> (Ballard 2002: 416)

Ballard's style is clinically exact, sparing with adjectives, metaphors and colour. Unlike Wells, he is not trying to generate wonder and excitement in the reader by transporting us to an undiscovered realm. His aim is to open our eyes, to make us see, in appalling detail, exactly what could be lying in store for us unless we take action in the present.

The traffic signs are Ballard's 'novum', the new element which generates a science-fiction story. Once you introduce a novum, it has to be combined with other new factors to make the idea plausible. So Ballard structures the near future around this central notion. Demolishing the argument that advertising widens choice, he establishes that there is only one brand of everything. Consumers trade in their car after three months even though the new one is exactly the same as the old. To convince us that the gigantic signs can cover the landscape unnoticed, Ballard's dystopia is dominated by the motorcar. Over a third of the land mass is covered by roads or parking areas, thick with traffic signs which camouflage any new construction. All of these interrelated elements complement each other in a vision of an automated, depersonalized society. It is not surprising that Franklin, like most of the population, is deeply conformist, swallowing the official line that subliminal advertising has been banned, and, in any case, has been proved ineffectual.

Franklin is another science-fiction 'everyman', leading a typically middle-class existence. He could have been any one of those men hunched over the wheel. In most dystopian fiction the protagonist rebels, making contact with an underground resistance. The narrative is resolved by his or her success or failure. Ballard's story follows this trajectory with great subtlety. Franklin is initially alerted to the signs by Hathaway, a local oddball. Despite overwhelming evidence, he still cannot fully accept Hathaway's claims. The story is punctuated by passages of dialogue between Hathaway and Franklin, debating the evidence for the conspiracy. Once again, dialogue is being used to liven up information the reader needs to know. This technique works in the 'yarn' although it might seem clunky in fiction that is more concerned with individual psychology.

Over forty years later, 'The Subliminal Man' seems uncannily prescient, especially in its account of an updated traffic system paradoxically in gridlock. Ballard has even foreseen the proliferation of television channels – each of them identical, apart from the commercials. In today's world women drivers might have joined the queue home from work, and we would use a credit card to pay the automat. But none of this detracts from the persuasiveness of Ballard's dystopian warning. He has simply pushed the available technology that bit further.

'Utopias', or perfect societies, occur less often in short fiction. It is easier to predict how much worse things might become than to imagine them all being set right. Science fiction is, according to Philip K. Dick, naturally inclined towards protest in an era where the planet is beset by war and suffering:

> In science fiction, a writer is not merely inclined to act out the Cassandra role; he is absolutely obliged to – unless, of course, he honestly thinks he will wake up some morning and find that the high-minded Martians have sneaked off with all our bombs and armaments, for our own good.
>
> (Dick 1995: 54)

Fiction depends on conflict; if something goes wrong in a perfect world, then by definition it is no longer perfect. In Ray Bradbury's ironic short tale 'There will Come Soft Rains' an automated house continues to anticipate its inhabitants' every need, preparing everything from morning pancakes to martinis and cigars in the evening. This is a Californian dream. But the house is no longer occupied. The family has been wiped out in a nuclear holocaust.

A dystopia is often a utopia gone wrong. In both Ballard's story and Bradbury's, human beings thought they had built a suburban paradise. Yet they destroyed themselves in the process, either figuratively through mindless consumerism or literally through warfare. Potentially a force for either good or evil, advances in technology still provoke debate, as we can see in current arguments concerning 'designer babies', genetically modified crops and global warming. Advances in computer technology, artificial intelligence and the World Wide Web have also had a huge impact on our daily lives and on the way we picture the future. This is the subject of the next section.

Cyberpunk: 'Burning Chrome' (William Gibson, 1981)

Cyberpunk derives its name from 'cybernetics', the comparative study of biological and artificial control systems – in other words, a fusion between machines and people, computers and brains. Cyberpunk writers use their imagination to play around with ideas about virtual reality, artificial intelligence and what it means to be human. Born in the USA but a permanent resident in Canada, William Gibson dreamt up the concepts of cyberspace and virtual reality after watching teenagers in video arcades. They were so wrapped up in the machines that they seemed to have entered an alternative world. His story 'Burning Chrome' maps out a vision that he has made his own, the vision he went on to explore in novels such as *Neuromancer*: 'It was hot, the night we burned Chrome. Out in the malls and plazas, moths were batting themselves to death against the neon, but in Bobby's loft the only light came from a monitor screen and the green and red LEDs on the face of the matrix simulator' (Shippey 2003: 496).

Science fiction needs to signal that we're entering another reality. A bold opening statement like this one commands the reader's attention; compare Philip K. Dick's 'He awoke – and wanted Mars' ('We Can Remember It For You Wholesale'). In both instances, we don't quite know what's going on. Who or what is 'Chrome', and what does 'burning' mean in this context? Malls, plazas and lofts are commonplace aspects of urban living, but the image of the moths adds exoticism to the familiar landscape.

Gibson has constructed a heightened version of today's global cities – frenetic and sprawling, a maze of clashing cultures, seedy, disreputable, potentially violent, yet also glamorous and seductive. But there have been countless other inputs, besides observation. Interviewed by Larry McCaffery, Gibson has spoken about the importance of music, especially Lou Reed and the Velvet Underground, and of the cult film *Escape from New York* in shaping his distinctive sensibility: 'Fiction, television, music, film – all provide material in the form of images and phrases and codes that creep into my writing in ways both deliberate and unconscious' (McCaffery 1990: 133). Becoming a writer means more than spending hours staring at words. It means getting out of that lonely room, opening up your eyes and ears, and exercising an insatiable curiosity.

Gibson glories in language. Slang expressions and technical jargon work themselves into his style, along with the words he has invented. The characters 'jack' into the system like junkies. They share the sensory experiences of their favourite 'simstim' stars ('simulated stimuli'). Aspiring stars head sometimes for Hollywood, more often for Chiba City, a name Gibson thought he made up but which really exists on the coast of Japan. Fact and fiction, fantasy and observation, are jumbled together so that sometimes it is impossible to tell them apart. Gibson has a jackdaw nature, adding random images and ideas to a story simply because they have caught his attention.

Like Wells, Gibson faces the problem of informing the reader. Where Wells conveys vital information through a relatively dry exchange of dialogue, Gibson introduces us to his fictional universe in descriptive passages, written in a hypnotic and rhythmical style:

> Bobby was a cowboy, Bobby was a cracksman, a burglar, casing mankind's extended electronic nervous system, rustling data and credit in the crowded matrix, monochrome nonspace where the only stars are dense concentrations of information, and high above it all burn corporate galaxies and the cold spiral arms of military systems.
>
> (Shippey 2003: 497)

The language is as tightly packed as the cities it describes. When the poet Baudelaire described the artist as a *flâneur* wandering the streets at random, absorbing whatever sensations came his or her way, he claimed that it was the sensory overload of the city that made it so intoxicating. This intoxication transmits itself to Gibson's energized prose. You may be reminded here of the vibrantly written letter I quoted from Katherine Mansfield in the activities for Chapter 2. Mansfield was also a *flâneur*, with her taste for dark cities and crowded cafés.

Modern SF blends all kinds of genres together. Gibson is able to borrow from the western and from detective fiction, balancing the difficulties of the story with other elements that are easier to grasp. The narrator introduces himself, Automatic Jack, and his associate, Bobby Quine, as comic-book characters: 'Bobby's the thin, pale dude with the dark glasses, and Jack's the mean-looking guy with the myoelectric arm' (Shippey 2003: 498). You can picture these two right away. The 'myoelectric arm' is less obvious, but its meaning soon emerges from the context. Gradually the reader pieces together all the slang words and technical phrases invented or borrowed by Gibson.

Chrome runs a massive database, which Bobby and Jack are attempting to access. She is a legendary figure, described in terms that, coincidentally, recall Wells's Abyss: 'with eyes that would have been at home on the bottom of some deep Atlantic trench, cold grey eyes that lived under terrible pressure' (Shippey 2003: 496–7). Scarcely human, her youthful appearance preserved by hormones, she is a powerful businesswoman, in cahoots with local gangsters. The stakes are very high. Bobby and Jack are risking their lives in order to steal a fortune.

The narrative is moved along by preparations for the heist and by a love triangle between Jack, Bobby and Bobby's girlfriend Rikki. Although the preparations are quite complicated, involving illegal software and backing from Macao, the basic plot is simple. Gibson is using a 'yarn' format to generate conflict and suspense – will they get away with it? Who will get the girl? By resorting to standard conventions, he's able to be more daring in his vision of the future. This is where the story's real interest lies. In recent years, plastic surgery has become relatively commonplace. This was only just beginning twenty years ago, when Gibson wrote 'Burning Chrome'. But in his fictional world, the human body is routinely modified. Rikki has had her corneas done twice, but she yearns for a more expensive pair of eyes. When she seduces Jack, she stimulates his prosthetic arm: 'And her hand went down the arm, black nails tracing a weld in the laminate, down to the black anodized elbow joint, out to the wrist, her hand soft-knuckled as a child's, fingers spreading to lock over mine, her palm against the perforated Duralumin' (Shippey 2003: 503).

Gibson expands on current trends. The street drug 'Vasopressin' does not sound so very far fetched. Designed to reverse forgetfulness in old age, its effect is to help you relive the past. Just as Borges resorted to fantasy to depict the true nature of his home town, Buenos Aires, Gibson sees his futuristic civilization as a rendition of present-day reality. He says 'my fiction amplifies and distorts *my* impressions of the world, however strange that world may be' (McCaffery 1990: 142).

The matrix itself is a multidimensional landscape which you can enter, thanks to the simulator: 'And down now, down, the program a roller coaster through this fraying maze of shadow walls, grey cathedral spaces between the bright towers. Headlong speed. Black ice. Don't think about it. Black ice' (Shippey 2003: 507).

We already know that the matrix is walled by 'ice' (standing for 'Intrusion Countermeasures Electronics', Shippey 2003: 497). The way in which Gibson extends this metaphor into the deadly 'black ice' shows the opportunities for wordplay and imagery in cyberfiction: 'Some kind of neural-feedback weapon, and you connect with it only once. Like some hideous Word that eats the mind from the inside out. Like an epileptic spasm that goes on and on until there's nothing left at all . . .' (Shippey 2003: 507).

As this is an adventure yarn, I will not give away the story's ending. But anyone who is familiar with the conventions of the hard-boiled detective story which has influenced Gibson might guess that a female character manages to hoodwink the hero. Gibson's work is further evidence that it is possible to make something original from intertextual influences, so long as these other voices are merged with your own.

Activity 1   Darkness

For this exercise I want you to step outside into the darkness. Not too far – and please don't go anywhere dangerous. Choose a quiet time of night, if possible. Stay still for around five or ten minutes, long enough to absorb the nocturnal atmosphere. How have shapes and textures changed? It is unlikely to be pitch black; what is the effect of moonlight or any other sort of light? Concentrate especially on noises and movement, close to you or far away. If it is summer you may be aware of insects or other creatures. Are there any smells that you associate with night-time? Is it cold or warm? Is there a breeze?

It is not essential to make notes. If you have one, you might like to record your impressions on a dictaphone. But it is more important to concentrate on the experience than to record it. Take a look at the shape and colour of the moon, and at the patterns of stars on a clear night. What do you think is out there in those distant galaxies? How would it feel to travel far into that darkness, not knowing if there would be a way back? What would it be like to look down on earth from space?

Describe the darkness. (You can go inside now if you wish!) You can concentrate on the nocturnal landscape close at home, or evoke the darkness of space, or even bring back a childhood fear of the dark, but make your description as real and as specific as you can. When you have finished, read some other descriptions of the darkness. For science-fiction examples, look at 'In the Avu Observatory' and 'The Cone' by H. G. Wells. To see how other writers have used night to create a special atmosphere, see the beginning of Elizabeth Bowen's 'Mysterious Kor' and the end of Nell Freudenberger's 'The Tutor'.

Activity 2   Another time, another place

For this exercise, you have been teleported across time and space. Don't worry about how or why or whether you'll get back. You can choose any time or place in the future or the past. Jot down your impressions at the moment you arrive. At this stage, historical accuracy is not important. Follow your instincts if you have chosen to go back in time. For instance, if you are in Elizabethan London, the first thing that strikes you could be the smell. People bathed very rarely in those days. If you have travelled to another planet, look around the landscape, not forgetting the sky.

Activity 3   Research

In the research activity at the end of Chapter 1, I advised you to cultivate the habits of the magpie, filching any material you can recycle into fiction. That advice holds good for speculative and science fiction. William Gibson has said that he fits an image, an idea or an expression into his work simply because it takes his fancy. As the writing progresses, patterns take shape by serendipity or some unconscious logic. Opening yourself to this kind of process makes the writing more exciting and, with any luck, the stories more dynamic. The thirst for knowledge stimulates creativity. Asked what sources would be most productive for new SF writers, Philip K. Dick gave this answer:

> Journals that deal in the most advanced research of clinical psychology, especially the work of the European existential analysis school. C. G. Jung. Oriental writings such as those on Zen Buddhism, Taoism, etc. Really authoritative – as compared with popularizations – historical works (e.g., *The Brutal Friendship*). Medieval works, especially those dealing with crafts, such as glass blowing – and science, alchemy, religion, etc. Greek philosophy, Roman literature of every sort. Persian religious texts. Renaissance studies on the theory of art. German dramatic writings of the Romantic period.
>
> (Dick 1995: 64–5)

Dick's idiosyncratic list reflects his own specialized interests. Philosophical, religious and psychological literature are especially relevant to a writer concerned with the nature of reality; how, for instance, could we tell the difference between our real memories and those implanted artificially? Dick considered this theme in 'We Can Remember It For You Wholesale', filmed as *Total Recall*. Studying remote historical periods and their civilizations can also alert us to cultures quite alien to contemporary Western values. In ancient Sparta, for instance, all free men were raised as warriors, even living with their army companions until the age of thirty when they were allowed to join their wives. Studying Spartan society gives you an insight into how any militarized culture might work in a fictional universe. You could even borrow specific elements, such as the slave class, the helots, who worked the land, supporting all those soldiers. What if, for instance, they were robots, or a supposedly inferior race? All civilizations fall eventually. What could be the downfall of your warrior caste?

Other items on the list are personal to Dick, and while an argument for their direct relevance to his work can be made I prefer to put the reading first. He read up on those subjects because he was drawn to them. And reading, as always, feeds into the writing. Find out what interests you.

There is also a more focused type of research which you will need to use occasionally in all types of fiction. This is the type of research which establishes factual information. The reading on Dick's list is ongoing, a constant source of inspiration. The second type of research is best carried out towards the end of the writing process. The risk in researching too much too early is that the story will be weighed down by the facts. When you have the information it is very difficult to resist including it, even though it may hold up the narrative. You will be surprised how far you can proceed by guesswork which later turns out to be correct. Being caught up imaginatively in your fictional world is more important in the first drafts than being 100 per cent accurate about the furniture. As I stressed at the beginning of the chapter, it is the creative concept which really counts when writing science fiction, not technical expertise. However, as part of the editing process you should check out anything you're not sure about in any type of story. Readers are distracted if you get the details wrong.

As an exercise in research skills, find a popular scientific magazine, such as *Nature* or *Scientific American* or collect newspaper articles on scientific issues, for example, cloning, space exploration or new technological gadgets. Choose an article about a scientific advance. This need not be an invention or technological process. The advance could be more theoretical, for instance ideas about the origins of the universe or the possibility of life on other planets. Make notes, using the following questions as guidelines:

1   What is the new advance? State it simply, in just one sentence.
2   What are the implications for the human race? Here you are thinking about what might be possible or what might have happened, even if this is just speculation.
3   Does the article say anything about what we do not know or what is impossible?
4   What do you think could be the next step after this one?

As a fiction writer you have an advantage over scientists who can only report well-established findings. You can make that leap from what can be proven to what can be imagined. If it can be imagined, it can be described. And if it can be described it can make a story.

Photocopy or make a careful note of where you found the article in case you want to refer to it again. You can follow up by pursuing other sources. Your library can advise you on electronic databases with access to news reports and articles. It is best to follow these avenues rather than use generalized search engines which do not discriminate.

Activity 4   The garden of forking paths

One of the great 'what ifs' asked by science fiction concerns the course of past history. Altering one historical fact changes present and future reality. Michael Moorcock's 'The Case of the Nazi Canary' (Chabon 2003) matches 'alternative history' with the classic detective yarn. If you read the opening exchanges between Sir Seaton Begg, 'metatemporal detective', and his sidekick John 'Taffy' Sinclair you will notice many similarities with Holmes and Watson (see Chapter 1). The pair are dispatched to Nazi Germany to investigate the suspicious death of Hitler's niece. In unravelling the mystery, Sir Seaton is complicit in the destruction of the Nazi party. Starting from a real event – the suicide of Geli Raubal – Moorcock has stopped Hitler in his tracks well before the outbreak of the Second World War.

Rewriting history changes our perspective on the past. Transformed into the whining, blotchy-faced 'Alf', Hitler is shorn of his previous mystique. Moorcock has created another type of 'parallel world' like those discussed in Chapter 4. The idea that life could take many different courses, depending on chance or a moment's decision, has become very familiar through recent films such as *Sliding Doors* and *Run, Lola, Run*. In Ray Bradbury's 'A Sound of Thunder', the whole of existence is changed when a time traveller treads on a butterfly. As Borges put it, 'Time forks perpetually towards innumerable futures' (Borges 1971: 53). On a smaller, more personal level you may sometimes have wondered how your life might have turned out if you hadn't gone to a particular party or studied a different subject. One small step leads to another in a whole chain of events.

For this exercise, ask yourself 'what if?' Staying with the idea of 'alternative history' rather than personal choices, let's shift reality a little. You don't have to get involved in political issues like Michael Moorcock, nor do you have necessarily to go far back in time. You could, for instance, take your cue from the urban legend that Elvis Presley is really alive. Invent a reality in which this is true, either because he took on another life or because you have changed the events surrounding his demise. How about if he went into politics like Reagan or Schwarzenegger? This is one activity which does require research from the beginning. You have to know the facts in order to change them.

Activity 5   Robots

The figure of the robot is very important to science fiction because robots make us consider the difference between a mechanical creature and a conscious being: what does it mean to be human? Can life be created artificially? Traditionally, robots replicate their makers, either as clumsy metallic forms or near-perfect imitations clothed in synthetic human skin. But they do not necessarily have to take human shape. Many devices already functioning as robots, for instance the space probes sent to investigate other planets, do not. In Gene Wolfe's 'How the Whip Came Back' (Shippey 2003), the robot secretary is a piece of reproduction furniture running on castors.

Imagine your own robot character. As in all the activities in this chapter, don't worry too much about originality. It is almost impossible to think up something that no one has ever thought of before, but you can develop a familiar idea, making it your own. Use the following questions to guide you:

- What is the robot's function? Robots usually do jobs which human beings cannot or do not want to do, often menial work or dangerous tasks; or they act as substitute pets or even children, as in Brian

Aldiss's 'Supertoys Last All Summer Long' (filmed as *AI*). What does your robot do?

- What does it (or she or he) look like? Is it humanoid? Form will tend to follow function, so the answer to the first question will partly determine the second. Be specific: if it's a dog, how big a dog?
- Does it have a name?
- Does it have a voice? How does it speak? Is it formal or chatty? Or does it have some other means of communicating?
- Is it one amongst many or a single prototype? Are robots cheap and commonplace or rare and valuable? Is it standard issue or an advanced model?
- Is it conscious? Does it have feelings? Does it have thoughts of its own? What is its attitude towards other robots, if there are any others, and towards human beings?

These questions may raise wide points about the fictional universe you are starting to create. As I pointed out in my discussion of 'The Subliminal Man', the original new idea or 'novum' (in this case, your robot) needs other new ideas to put it in operation.

In 'Runaround' Isaac Asimov formulated his influential three laws of robotics. Given in the original story as dialogue, these are the three rules which robots are programmed to obey:

1   A robot may not injure a human being or, through inaction, allow a human being to come to harm.
2   A robot must obey the orders given to it by human beings except where such orders would conflict with the First Law.
3   A robot must protect its own existence as long as such protection does not conflict with the First or Second Laws.

Conflict comes about when, for instance, a robot is instructed to participate in warfare. In 'Runaround', Asimov's robot is used to mine for a precious mineral on Mercury, where outside temperatures would kill a human being. Because of the extreme conditions, the Third Law has been programmed more forcibly than usual. A situation arises in which the contradictions in the rules seem irresolvable, and the robot is literally running round in circles.

Use the laws to develop a story involving your own robot character.

Outline the premise and the basic situation. The resolution can be saved for later.

Activity 6   The novum

In the previous two exercises, you have roughed out some story ideas based on different kinds of science-fiction 'novum'. In this chapter we have touched on other kinds of story ideas which provide a basic story-telling template. Working on these ideas will help you to think about narrative structure as well as generating plots you can use. You can combine the following categories if you wish.

New invention

A thought-reading device? A faster way to travel? Make up your own invention or technological process, and think about the social implications. You may already have some ideas, following the research activities I suggested earlier. As I have stressed, it is the human factor which makes the story interesting, rather than the hardware. For instance, in 'Love Alters' by the British writer Tanith Lee (Green and Lefanu 1985), scientists have found a way to make female eggs or male sperm fertilize each other. In a future where homosexuality is the norm and hetero-sexuality abhorrent, this allows same-sex marriages to reproduce. Lee does not bother explaining how this is done: 'I have never grasped the mechanics', her narrator says blithely (Green and Lefanu 1985: 63). The narrative arises out of the human conflict that occurs when she falls in love with a man. This unpredictable human response to the conditions brought about by the change is one strategy for developing the narrative. Another possibility is to think about what happens when the machine or the process malfunctions.

Utopia/dystopia

Incubating babies outside the womb may be your idea of a perfect world or your idea of hell. As we have seen, science fiction tends more towards dystopias, possibly reflecting the pessimistic times we live in. How do you envisage a perfect society? Is it possible to eliminate, or at least reduce, violence, greed and inequality? Who would make the rules and how would they be enforced? Your utopia could be set on another planet, or in the future on earth, or even in a colony or space station. A good way to structure the utopian story is to make it a traveller's tale, told from the viewpoint of an outsider. You can then contrast the utopia with our own or a similar culture. As in the 'island' activities in the previous chapter, you will need to indicate how the visitor has arrived and why they are there.

Alien encounter

Perhaps the human race is incapable of perfection, and you peopled your utopia with another species. In the examples from Wells, Martin, Arthur C. Clarke and Le Guin, we have glimpsed a wide range of alien life forms, from creatures who would seem to be our close relations to beings who have more in common physically with insects or reptiles. One source of inspiration is, in fact, to visit your nearest zoo or aquarium, or watch a natural-history programme such as David Attenborough's BBC series, *The Living Planet*. Even here on earth, life forms have adapted to their environment in extraordinary ways. Write a report on a newly discovered species. You will need to consider both its differences and its similarities to the human race, and the conditions in which it can thrive. You might base your report on the classifications near the start of Le Guin's 'Semley's Necklace'. This is an extract from the '*Abridged Handy Pocket Guide to Intelligent Life-Forms*': '*A. Gdemiar (singular Gdem): Highly intelligent, fully hominoid nocturnal troglodytes. 120–35 cm in height, light skin, dark head-hair. When contacted these cave-dwellers possessed a rigidly stratified oligarchic urban society modified by partial colonial telepathy, and a technologically oriented Early Steel culture*' (Shippey 2003: 322).

Apocalypse

As Ballard suggested, SF delivers a graphic reminder of the horrors yet to come if we ignore the warnings. In Bradbury's 'There will Come Soft Rains', humanity is wiped out by nuclear warfare, but there are plenty of other candidates for a doomsday scenario, including ecological disaster. Following Bradbury's strategy, describe the aftermath. Detached understatement works better than shovelling out the gore. In Bradbury's story, the absence of the human beings is more effective than a full account of how they met their grisly end.

Activity 7   Beginnings

Science fiction is very good at attention-grabbing openings. It is also very good at putting you into the picture quickly. There have already been several examples in this chapter. The first sentence of Clarke's 'Second Dawn' signals an alien race: ' "Here they come," said Eris, rising to his forefeet and turning to look down the long valley' (Shippey 2003: 198). Tanith Lee's 'Love Alters' plays with ambiguity about gender in the 'I' pronoun: 'I had been married to Jenny for two whole years when I fell in love with a man' (Green and Lefanu 1985: 60).

Short fiction in general is a concise form. Stories get straight down to business. Both of these openings are crisp and decisive, yet they also raise questions in the reader's mind. They make us curious. Most short stories begin with some sort of dynamic opening. As I have already suggested, they rarely waste time simply setting the scene. When background information is essential, as it often is in science fiction, we are acquainted with the minimum we need to know as painlessly as possible. Description is integrated with a character's actions or thoughts, or intercut with speech. Short stories tend to introduce dialogue into the narrative much more quickly than novels. In 'yarns', including science fiction, key information is often transmitted through dialogue, though you should beware of this technique in less plot-driven stories. Using one of the ideas outlined in the previous exercise, write an opening sentence. It should be short and to the point, and hook the reader immediately.

Activity 8   Journey into the Unknown

We began this chapter with H. G. Wells's underwater expedition, a proto-type for many other science-fiction tales, notably the journey into space. But the concept of a journey has wider applications in the short story. A narrative is a type of mental journey for the reader, the writer and often for the characters. To make a story, something has to move. Something has to have changed by the ending, even if the change only lies in an awareness that life has stayed the same.

For this exercise, imagine a character is going on a difficult journey. They could be travelling into space or just crossing the road, but they are travelling alone, and are not sure what they will find. You can write either first- or third-person narrative. Begin by suggesting your character's thoughts and feelings as they set out on that journey. This is a journey for you too. I want you to discover the story as you write rather than mapping it out beforehand. Write for between twenty and thirty minutes. Your character should not yet have reached their destination.

Now place an obstacle in their way. This could be anything from a technical hitch to a personal problem. Something threatens their chances of reaching their goal. It is up to you to decide if they reach their destination. Finish the draft as quickly as you can. If you are writing science fiction, look again at my discussion of 'In the Abyss' when you have completed your first draft. For this exercise you have written a linear story in a linear way, starting at the beginning and moving straight on to the end. Remember, stories don't always have to start at the beginning, and you don't have to write the beginning first. Some writers work towards an ending which is already clear in their mind. As you work at the exercises, try and identify your own creative habits and work with them, bringing out the best in your writing.

6

Reality

Very few of us are able to devote long stretches of time to our writing. Most of us snatch moments between work, family, study and other responsibilities, leading lives that are hardly conducive to long sustained projects. If this is your situation Raymond Carver's account may well strike a chord:

> In those days I figured if I could squeeze in an hour or two for myself, after job and family, that was more than good enough. That was heaven itself. And I felt happy to have that hour. But sometimes, one reason or another, I couldn't get the hour. Then I would look forward to Saturday, though sometimes things happened that knocked Saturday out as well. But there was Sunday to hope for. Sunday; maybe.
>
> (Carver 1994: 35)

His solution became 'Get in, get out. Don't linger. Go on' (Carver 1994: 22). Yet, as Carver soon makes plain, he won't be rushed. The short story lends itself to irregular, intensive bursts of writing. It gives you the satisfaction of producing completed pieces of work within a foreseeable time frame. But writing short stories also demands extreme precision. In a condensed form, every word counts. Carver's methods involve scrupulous redrafting, paring down and polishing until every last comma is in the right place. He forges his artistic practice out of necessity, as he fits the writing to his lifestyle, and turns his limitations into virtues.

Another advantage of short fiction is its ability to respond to changing circumstances. Carver makes the contrast with the novel: 'To write a novel, it seemed to me, a writer should be living in a world that makes sense, a world that the writer can believe in, draw a bead on, and then write about accurately. A world that will, for a time anyway, stay fixed in one place' (Carver 1994: 35). Carver is talking mostly about the insecurities in his own life, as he struggles through various dead-end jobs. But he's also suggesting that short fiction engages with a fragmented society more easily than the traditional novel. The men and women he describes in stories like 'Boxes' move back and forth between jobs, homes and relationships, making the best of these temporary arrangements:

> I like where I live. I didn't when I first moved here. There was nothing to do at night, and I was lonely. Then I met Jill. Pretty soon, after a few weeks, she brought her things over and started living with me. We didn't set any long-term goals. We were happy and we had a life together. We told each other we'd finally got lucky. But my mother didn't have anything going in her life. So she wrote me and said she'd decided on moving here.
>
> (Carver 1998: 335)

The term 'dirty realism' was coined to describe writers such as Carver, Richard Ford and Jayne Anne Phillips, who dealt with contemporary America in plain, down-to-earth language. Their work was often regarded as grim and depressing, but this is to miss the laconic humour in passages such as this. Carver makes everyday life extraordinary by simply lingering to look and to listen. One of his favourite images is of the light in a neighbour's house, and this is the image which closes 'Boxes': 'What's there to tell? The people over there embrace for a minute, and then they go inside the house together. They leave the light burning. Then they remember, and it goes out' (Carver 1998: 346).

In Chapter 2, I discussed the relationship between still photography and the short story. Once again, the instant is recorded by the mind's eye – this time, perhaps, more like a movie camera.

Grace Paley has also adapted short fiction to her lifestyle, combining a writing career with her role as a political activist, notably in the peace movement. Almost all of her stories are set within New York's Lower East Side where she has spent most of her life. Characters recur, including her first-person narrators, Faith and Virginia, who have aged and developed alongside their creator. Reading Paley's three collections takes you inside a virtual neighbourhood, overlapping the real one. Her playful style has grown out of her multilingual background. She was raised in an immigrant household where Russian, Yiddish and English were used interchangeably. Like William Gibson (discussed in the previous chapter), she is fascinated by street slang. In 'The Pale Pink Roast', Peter says, 'You look like a chick on the sincere make. Playing it cool and living it warm' (Paley 1980: 47). As she herself comments, 'This language of ours, here in this country, is always being refreshed and scrambled and knocked around. It's always coming up from the bottom, again and again' (Isaacs 1990: 125). She has also said, 'I couldn't write stories, really, until I really heard – *listened* – to enough other voices and tried to make that *stretch* to other voices. Then I really found my own' (Isaacs 1990: 120).

Paley's prose is fancier than Carver's so-called 'minimalism' – richer in metaphors and word play. But both have absorbed the living, spoken language in which we are submerged. In their different ways, both produce accessible and vivid stories. It can be difficult to switch between the formal, impersonal language we are expected to use in essays and report-writing to the type of language that comes naturally in speech but is often frowned upon when it is set down on paper. If you write with the language you speak and you think with, you are drawing on endless reserves of energy to fuel your storytelling.

Quick to produce and relatively simple to publish, through readings, anthologies and pamphlets, the short story provides an outlet for suppressed voices. The Federation of Worker Writers and Community Publishers supports groups in Britain and the USA who see writing as a means of empowering their local community. The British-based Peepal Tree Press is raising awareness of a Caribbean tradition in short fiction, upheld by writers such as Oliver Senior, Merle Collins, V. S. Naipaul, Wilson Harris and Pauline Melville.

In his study *The Lonely Voice*, Frank O'Connor claimed that the short story belonged to outsiders, and that marginalized cultures were supreme in short fiction – a view borne out if you consider Ireland (James Joyce, Elizabeth Bowen, William Trevor), Russia (Chekhov, Gorky, Tolstoy) or the southern states of America (Eudora Welty, William Faulkner, Flannery O'Connor). In his foreword to Alistair MacLeod's collection of stories set in Cape Breton, Nova Scotia, John McGahern – himself a chronicler of life in rural Ireland – echoes Carver's comparison with the novel:

> I think of the novel as the most social of all the art forms, the most closely linked to an idea of society, a shared leisure, and a system of manners. The short story does not generally flourish in such a society but comes into its own like song or prayer or superstition in poorer more fragmented communities where individualism and tradition and family and localities and chance or luck are dominant.
>
> (MacLeod 2002: xiii–xiv)

This is true of MacLeod's stories, as it is of the British writer Panos Karnezis's tales of a fictional Greek village in his *Little Infamies* collection.

But the short story is also bang up to the minute. There could be no better medium for the age of the text message, the sound byte and the short attention span. In the twenty-first century news travels fast. Communications are speeded up, and the pace of change accelerates relentlessly. The short story has the flexibility to capture the heat of the moment. A short, compressed form captures the intensity of contemporary urban life, as we have seen in the work of William Gibson. Short stories are also able to engage with events as they arise; in the years it takes to get a novel published, the world has moved on, and today's breaking news is ancient history.

Back in the 1960s, Joyce Carol Oates wrote 'Where Are You Going, Where Have You Been?' after reading about the serial killer Charles Schmid in *Life* magazine and also after listening to the Bob Dylan song 'It's All Over Now, Baby Blue'. By entering into the mind of the victim, Oates penetrates the subject matter far more deeply than was possible in the original article. By taking a subjective viewpoint, fiction makes us empathize with characters who are just names and images in the daily news. To some extent, we have to anaesthetize ourselves to the terrible events in the headlines, or else we'd be crippled by anguish and horror. The insight Oates gives us into how it might feel to slowly realize you've been trapped by a sex killer is absolutely terrifying. Almost forty years later, the story is just as powerful; it is of its time but has a universal resonance.

Alice Walker's 'The Abortion' reflects her own involvement in the black civil rights and women's liberation movements in the USA. Her protagonist's experiences neatly illustrate the dilemmas facing women after abortion was legalized, identifying an imbalance of power between men and women both within marriage and in society at large. The story touches on the impact of desegregation in schools and also raises awareness of environmental issues. The heroine has been deeply affected by her mother's death from lung cancer, caused by asbestos, and she is initially opposed to air-conditioning. In fact, there are very few aspects of her life that are not connected to political struggles. Walker's writing is polemical; she believes that fiction has a responsibility to change public attitudes.

In her 1991 Nobel prize-winner's lecture, the South African short-story writer and novelist Nadine Gordimer said that the writer's duty was first of all to the writing. By writing honestly and well, the writer is already taking the side of freedom. Your writing will always be shaped by your own society. As she put it, referring to repressive states such as apartheid South Africa, 'the writer's themes and characters inevitably are formed by the pressures and distortions of that society as the life of the fisherman is determined by the power of the sea' (Gordimer 1991).

In the close readings in this chapter, I shall introduce two different approaches to capturing reality. The first is social observation, documenting everyday life. This is exemplified by the nineteenth-century French writer, Guy de Maupassant. The second is personal testimony, capturing first-hand experience through autobiographical styles of writing. My example here comes from the Canadian Alice Munro. Before discussing Maupassant's 'Country Living', I should like to look more broadly at the connections between the short story and journalism, which will be especially relevant when you make your own attempts at social observation.

The short story and journalism

It was a delivery driver who first noticed the wooden box left at the junction of Sixth and Byrd streets in Little Rock, Arkansas on May 14. It bore the warning 'Live Venomous Reptiles', and as he moved the lid to peer in, a large cobra lifted its head to strike.

> The country postman, Médéric Rompel, whom everyone round-about called Médéri for short, left the post office at Roüy-le-Tors at his usual time. Striding through the town with the military step of an old soldier, he first cut across the fields at Villaumes before reaching the banks of the Brindille and following its course which led him to the village of Carvelin where his round began.

Each of these openings draws in the reader, using techniques drawn from the old-fashioned yarn. Each creates suspense through painstaking reconstruction, sharpening our anticipation with every little detail. The mysterious package is a familiar device, dating back to the legend of Pandora's box which I included as an activity in Chapter 1. The second extract builds more slowly towards its revelation; but, as you may have suspected, Médéri does not simply finish his round and head back home again.

The first extract comes from a report in a British newspaper, headlined 'Deadly Snakes Link to Mysterious Death of Briton in US' (*Guardian*, 24 May 2004). The writer, Kirsty Scott, quotes from a local zookeeper: 'I thought, holy cow! We've got some pretty serious animals'. This is pretty much stating the obvious – nothing here we couldn't guess. But she has included this little speech because it adds colour and character, just like the dialogue in a fictional story.

The second example is taken from Guy de Maupassant's story 'The Little Roque Girl'. Like the newspaper journalist, Maupassant establishes a 'factual' record, starting with a specific time and place. He gives the postman's full name and retraces his route through the village, maintaining a dispassionate observational tone as events unfold. On his way through the woods, Médéri makes a shocking discovery: 'It was a little girl of perhaps 12. Her arms were wide open, her legs were spread apart, and her face was covered by a handkerchief. A small quantity of blood was spattered on her thighs' (Maupassant 1990: 204).

As the scene is recreated, the account shades inevitably into the post-man's reactions: 'He could not fathom it. Was she asleep, perhaps?' (Maupassant 1990: 204). The *Guardian* report also notes the bafflement of the Arkansas police after the man who ordered the snakes was found dead half a mile away from the junction where the driver opened the box. Journalism relies on eyewitness reports and expert opinion in the drive towards accuracy. In each case, the whole truth is a matter for conjecture.

Journalism and the short story are closely related. Maupassant himself was a working journalist, who turned out a constant stream of articles as well as 300 stories, crossing many different genres. Ernest Hemingway, Ruth Rendell, Mavis Gallant and Gabriel García Márquez are just a few of the other great story writers to have honed their skills in the trade. Journalism teaches concision and structure. Journalists learn how to bring the facts to life with carefully selected details – the cobra lifting its head, the face covered by a hankie. These lessons stand them in good stead when they turn to writing fiction. The basic techniques of story-telling apply across the board. The short story is a very flexible form, crossing into non-fiction. The British literary magazine *Granta* mingles travel writing, reportage, memoirs and essays with stories and extracts from novels. It is often hard to distinguish between categories. Anna Funder's *Stasiland: Stories From Behind the Berlin Wall*, a mosaic of individual experiences from the former East Germany, uses techniques you might expect in a short-story collection. As I pointed out in Chapter 3, comic writing often straddles the boundary between fiction and journalism, in the form of the humorous sketch or anecdote, as practised by James Thurber, P. G. Wodehouse, Dorothy Parker, Mark Twain, Stephen Leacock – and not forgetting Garrison Keillor.

A background in journalism provides another important benefit, in addition to a training in narrative technique; it brings home an awareness of addressing an audience. You are communicating much more directly with your readership than is usually the case in writing fiction. You are writing with a clear purpose in mind, whether it is to inform, entertain or argue a viewpoint, and you will often provoke an active response. If you have written so much as a review in a student newspaper you will recognize the experience. Writing for publication adds focus to your writing and develops confidence under pressure. Even participating in a writers' workshop can have this effect.

The British writer Graham Greene once said that all writing is a form of therapy: 'sometimes I wonder how all those who do not write, compose or paint can manage to escape the madness, the melancholia, the panic fear which is inherent in the human situation' (Greene 1980: 275). But if you only write to please yourself the results will be too inward-looking to succeed artistically. Greene also said that every writer has a splinter of ice in their heart (Greene 1999). Keeping a clear eye and a cool sense of detachment can only benefit your writing. These qualities are instilled in good journalists and in the best fiction writers.

I am not suggesting that becoming a professional journalist is essential for every short-story writer. But, as well as learning journalistic skills, you should consider any outlets for your writing, including those for non-fiction. There are many more readers of newspapers and magazines than there are for the literary journals in which most fiction writers make their debut. People are fascinated by true stories. The idea that something actually happened is extremely compelling, especially when we're hearing it from the horse's mouth. That is why Funder's *Stasiland* has been so successful amongst British readers. Newspapers and magazines often ask readers to contribute short pieces based on real-life experiences. The British *Sunday Telegraph Magazine* asks 'Do You Have a Story to Tell?', inviting non-fiction submissions of around 600 words. If you read these short articles you will find the material is crafted exactly like a short story. Eric Cottam's 'King of the Road' begins tantalizingly with the following sentence: 'Some of our members may remember him, our temporary coach-driver at the British Limbless Ex-Service Men's Association Home in Crieff, during that long, hot summer a few years back' (*Sunday Telegraph Magazine*, 11 July 2004).

Cottam's story is a character sketch, complete with dialogue, and with a twist at the end: the burly, tattooed driver reveals that he collects thimbles as a hobby. It could easily be published as a piece of fiction.

Truth can seem like fiction, and fiction seem like truth. The difference is not so much in the material itself as in the context and the way it is presented. We saw in Chapter 1 how even the most far-fetched yarn can suspend our disbelief with the aid of eyewitness accounts and 'documentary' evidence. In this chapter we are not so much concerned with these techniques as with looking at writing which is avowedly realistic, which tries to present a true record of life as it is lived. As you will discover, this is not a simple undertaking. There are many versions of reality, as Nabokov pointed out (see Chapter 4). Some postmodern thinkers deny that there can ever be such a thing as the unvarnished truth. This is not the place for high theory, though we will touch on such questions in the section on autobiographical writing. In the rest of the chapter I am concerned with the two practical aspects of writing short fiction: firstly, the techniques writers use to represent the world we live in, and secondly the strategies they draw upon to convince us that their stories are 'realistic'. We start the investigation with another Maupassant story, 'Country Living'.

Social observation: 'Country Living' (Guy de Maupassant, 1882)

Like 'The Little Roque Girl', 'Country Living' is written in an impersonal narrative voice, using an omniscient narrator. At first glance, it seems to be a straightforward factual account of the lives of French peasants towards the end of the nineteenth century:

> The two cottages stood side by side at the foot of a hill not far from a small spa town. The two peasant farmers who lived in them worked very hard cultivating the poor soil to rear all the children they had. Each couple had four, and outside each house the whole gang of them played and shrieked from morning till night. The two oldest were 6 and the two youngest about fifteen months. Weddings and then births had occurred at more or less the same times in both houses.
>
> (Maupassant 1990: 90)

These are typical families, whose lives follow a preordained pattern. But this pattern is disrupted when a rich couple, the d'Hubières, take a fancy to the children. They decide to adopt one. The first family they approach are taken aback and reject the offer. Having phrased their proposal more carefully, they are successful with the second. The family who have kept their son envy the prosperity their neighbours' deal has brought them, but also become loudly self-righteous about their own decision. When the adopted boy, now grown up, comes visiting in his smart carriage, the other young man berates his parents for not giving him away instead and storms out of their hovel.

The detached third-person narration gives the impression that Maupassant is merely documenting reality. Every sentence in that opening paragraph is a simple statement, without ornamentation and without comment. He pays close attention to accuracy, especially in numbers and quantities, listing the contents of the family meal – 'a bowl containing bread soaked in the water the potatoes had been boiled in, half a cabbage, and three onions'. But of course this 'documentary' is a highly crafted work of fiction. However authentic these details may be as a record of living conditions, they have been arranged to suit his purpose. When he informs us that Madame d'Hubières's pockets are 'bulging with sweeties and pennies' (Maupassant 1990: 91), the contrast between the two lifestyles could not be more clear.

133

Although 'Country Living' is solidly based on observation, it is written primarily to entertain. Maupassant dramatizes the situation, putting words into his characters' mouths. This fast-moving interchange follows the visit from the pampered young man. Charlot, the boy left behind with his family, looks on with resentment:

That night, at supper, he said to his parents: 'You can't have been right in the head letting the Vallin kid get took away.'
His mother replied stubbornly: 'I'd never have let a child of ours get took.'
His father said nothing.
The son went on: 'I really missed the boat the day I got made a sacrifice of.'

(Maupassant 1990: 95)

The dialogue is so well paced we can hear the hesitations and silences. It also rings true. Maupassant's story would transfer very easily to stage or screen because it is told externally, through speech, gesture and visual details – for instance, when he describes how Charlot's mother would pick up the little boy, declaring, 'I din't sell you, my precious, I din't! I don't go round selling my children.' (Maupassant 1990: 94).

Maupassant's characters are all social types. In the opening passage, the peasant families are interchangeable, and as the story unfolds their differences stem from their changed circumstances rather than from innate personal qualities. There is no meaning and no moral message. It all comes down to chance. In this respect, the story stays true to life. Unlike real life, it is shaped very clearly by cause and effect. The narrative follows a linear chain of events set in motion by the intervention of the wealthy couple. While the exact consequences are unpredictable, they still succeed each other logically. In life, it's much more difficult to pinpoint causality. When does a relationship start to deteriorate? What makes an individual choose one job over another? Maupassant himself said that 'the realist, if he is an artist, will endeavour not to show us a banal photograph of life, but to provide us with a vision that is at once more complete, more startling, and more convincing than reality itself' (Maupassant 2001: 7). Art consists of 'bringing to light essential events by literary skill alone while giving others their due, depending on their significance, in order to create the desired profound sense of special truth' (Maupassant 2001: 8).

As Maupassant acknowledges, all illusions are sustained artificially. To be accepted as 'realistic', the characters and events in a short story need to be much more sharply defined than they would appear in real life. This 'craft of composition' is especially evident in the plot reversals at the end of 'Country Living'. All our assumptions are turned inside out. Previously Charlot has been proud of his family for not selling him; now he blames them for not giving him a better life. The parents have made the decision to keep him, only to lose him as a consequence. At the very moment when their own son disappears forever, they can hear their next-door neighbours celebrating their lucky lad's return.

Maupassant never gets close to his characters. They are not complex individuals, like the characters in Joyce Carol Oates's story; although we might feel compassion, we do not empathize with them, like we do with Connie, the girl who is trapped by the killer. We never feel as if we're in their shoes. Maupassant studies human behaviour from the outside, like a scientist observing apes or insects. This is why the term 'naturalism' is often applied to his work, alongside novels and stories by other French writers of the time, such as Flaubert and Zola. But to put us completely in the picture he hints at the psychological motivations behind external actions. When Madame d'Hubières first spots the children her husband stays silent 'for he was used to these sudden enthusiasms which he felt as a physical hurt and took more or less as a personal reproach' (Maupassant 1990: 91). From this evidence we understand that Madame is to be indulged while Monsieur will endure anything for the sake of a quiet life. And that is the way he remains for the rest of the story. He is psychologically consistent.

This psychological consistency is something we have come to expect from fictional characters. Contemporary short stories based on social observation tend to explore characters in greater depth than Maupassant's brief vignettes. 'Winterscape' by the Indian writer Anita Desai also involves the 'borrowing' of children. The story describes two Indian sisters. Asha, her father's favourite, is blessed with beauty and charm, while Anu is rather mousy. Yet when they marry it is Anu rather than Asha who proves to be fertile. When Asha's husband is killed preparing to host a party for Anu's first-born, Anu consoles Asha by letting her keep the child, in the full expectation that she will have more children. A few years later, Anu's own husband dies. She moves in with her sister, assuming the role of an aunt. This complex family history is recounted by the son, Rakesh, to his wife in Canada as they await a visit from both 'mothers'. Herself a new mother, Beth is already dreading the ordeal. Now she realizes how distant Rakesh's culture is from her own Western values. Focalizing the story mostly through Beth, Desai deals even-handedly with the cultural divide. Like Maupassant, she resists moral judgements.

Social observation need not be unrelentingly grim. Detachment can sometimes be tempered by humour and compassion. Much of Desai's work could be classified as social comedy. This is an area I discussed in Chapter 3, but it is worth emphasizing that, well handled, a story's tone can shift between moods. In 'Royalty', an elderly couple's summer is blighted when an old friend and literary celebrity outstays his welcome. The nuances of upper-class Indian politeness are anatomized in excruci-ating detail, yet the story ends on a dying fall as the couple finally make their escape to the cool of the Himalayas:

> When she reached the rock where he was waiting, she sank down onto it and wiped her face with the corner of her sari. 'I can't do these climbs any more', she admitted, with a wince. 'You had better do them alone.'
>
> 'Oh, Sarla,' he said, catching up her hand in his, 'I would never want to come up here without you, you know.'
>
> (Desai 2001: 23)

Humour and melancholy are finely balanced. Characters like Ravi and Sarla, whose life has somehow passed them by, are more interesting to writers than characters who have found worldly success. After all, in 'Country Living', Maupassant focuses on Charlot, leaving the adopted boy on the sidelines. The Canadian Mavis Gallant's gift for social observation also settles on characters who, socially speaking, have missed the boat, for reasons they cannot quite understand. In 'The Ice Wagon Going Down the Street', all her expatriate couple have to show for their time working in Europe is an outdated Paris dress: 'The Balenciaga is their talisman, their treasure; and after they remember it they touch hands and think that the years are not behind them but hazy and marvelous and still to be lived' (Gallant 2004: 193).

In the introduction to his collection *Under the Banyan Tree*, the Indian writer R. K. Narayan describes finding inspiration for his stories roaming the streets and markets of Mysore. He extols the sheer joy of observation and listening in to conversations. Short stories, he says, are the best medium for utilizing this huge wealth of material. Unlike novels which pursue a central theme, 'short stories [. . .] can cover a wider field by presenting concentrated miniatures of human experience in all its opulence' (Narayan 1987: viii). You will never run out of ideas once you start looking and listening.

Memories: 'Family Furnishings' (Alice Munro, 2001)

Your memories are an invaluable storehouse of imagery and experience. Many of the activities I have included in earlier chapters draw their material from this powerful source. I often encourage new writers to start with autobiography. Once you get going, one memory sparks off another, and the page fills up almost automatically. Some people turn to autobiography to make sense of their life, without any thought of publication. For those who take their writing more seriously, the craft of putting the story together takes over from the original therapeutic impulse. As the American Lorrie Moore puts it, 'writing is both the excursion into and the excursion out of one's life' (Boylan 1993: 202).

The Canadian short-story writer Alice Munro describes her work as 'personal' rather than strictly autobiographical. Several collections have been prefaced by a disclaimer, explaining that their content is purely fictional. But while there is no exact correspondence between the events in the stories and biographical fact, her stories often parallel her own experiences. The narrator in 'Family Furnishings' (Munro 2001) shares much in common with the author. Her mother dies prematurely from an illness resembling Parkinson's disease; growing up in small-town Ontario, she wins a two-year scholarship, dropping college to get married when the award runs out. She also becomes a writer. Munro can write about how it feels to live through these experiences because she has done it herself, but we cannot assume that every detail is factually accurate.

What Munro does is use the conventions of autobiographical writing to investigate ways in which we manipulate the truth, both in writing and in everyday life. Her work is all about the stories we tell one another and the tales we tell ourselves. Like 'straight' autobiography, 'Family Furnishings' is told retrospectively by a first-person narrator. It begins with a vivid family anecdote:

> Alfrida. My father called her Freddie. The two of them were first
> cousins and lived on adjoining farms and then for a while in the

same house. One day they were out in the fields of stubble playing with my father's dog, whose name was Mack. That day the sun shone, but did not melt the ice in the furrows. They stomped on the ice and enjoyed its crackle underfoot.

(Munro 2001: 86)

An ordinary day – but especially memorable because it marked the end of the First World War. This is the type of anecdote that often does the rounds at family gatherings. But already Munro sounds a note of caution as the narrator's father chips in: 'How could she remember a thing like that? my father said. She made it up, he said' (Munro 2001: 86).

Compare Alfrida's anecdote with the news item about the snakes on p. 129. Can we be sure the delivery driver saw the cobra poised to strike as he lifted the lid? Or did it simply make a better story told that way? Equally, the tale might have been embellished by the newspaper. But you can be fairly sure that when he repeats that story to his grandchildren he will always envisage that dramatic moment.

Munro's narrator goes on to record her own memories of Alfrida, a 'career girl' who worked on a regional paper. Some of her memories are generalized: 'Washing and drying the dishes, in the kitchen, the aunts would talk about who had a tumor, a septic throat, a bad mess of boils. They would tell about how their own digestions, kidneys, nerves were functioning' (Munro 2001: 91).

The use of 'would' signals regular, repeated actions. The narrator is acting as an oral historian, explaining how people lived in those days. But 'would' is a clumsy construction, blunting the sentence, and needs to be restricted. In this next extract, Munro has replaced 'would talk' and 'would tell' with 'talked' and 'told':

While we worked in the kitchen Alfrida talked to me about celebrities – actors, even minor movie stars, who had made stage appearances in the city where she lived. In a lowered voice still broken by wildly disrespectful laughter she told me stories of their bad behavior, the rumors of private scandals that had never made it into the magazines.

(Munro 2001: 95)

These generalized memories are punctuated by one-off incidents typifying Alfrida's place in the narrator's life – Alfrida encouraging her to smoke or to mimic her elders – often including brief snatches of dialogue. During the period of her mother's rapid decline, Alfrida's visits tail off. She may have been avoiding the atmosphere of the sickbed, but, with hindsight, the narrator speculates about other possible reasons:

> It may have been that Alfrida asked if she could bring her friend and had been told that she could not. If she was already living with him, that would have been one reason, and if he was the same man she had later, the fact that he was married would have been another.

(Munro 2001: 98)

Throughout the story, Munro is showing us how the past is reinterpreted when we look back from the vantage point of the present. She is also suggesting that this sort of speculation, like gossip and hearsay, is spurred on by a natural storytelling impulse. For some people, like the narrator herself, this turns into an artistic vocation. But the fiction-making process is something we all take part in without even noticing.

In Chapter 2, I said that the short story usually tackles a more concentrated time span than novels, which unfold over longer stretches of time. 'Family Furnishings' overcomes this problem with a shifting time frame, able to jump from one period in the character's life to another. The narrative shoots forwards from the narrator's girlhood to her time at college and then to her present life as a writer. The holes this leaves in the narrative are known as 'ellipses' (singular 'ellipsis'). Short-story writers use ellipses to condense the narrative and skip irrelevant explanations. When the narrator mentions 'I had ended my marriage for personal – that is, wanton – reasons' (Munro 2001: 113) that is all we need to know. There's no reason to get bogged down in background information.

Munro's unnamed narrator goes to college in the city where Alfrida lives. Finally accepting a dinner invitation, she listens to Alfrida's version of another, more unsettling family legend. This is the story of how Alfrida's mother died from burns after an accident with an oil lamp. Alfrida confides that she had begged in vain to see her mother on her deathbed. A phrase Alfrida remembers repeating at that time sticks in the narrator's own memory:

> It was as if a trap had snapped shut, to hold those words in my head. I did not exactly understand what use I would have for them.

139

> I only knew how they jolted me and released me, right away, to breathe a different kind of air, available only to myself.
>
> *She would want to see me.*
>
> (Munro 2001: 111)

That phrase and the images associated with it – 'the exploding lamp, the mother in her charnel wrappings, the staunch, bereft child' (Munro 2001: 113) are stored away until years later they surface in a story about an entirely different character. The narrator has almost forgotten their origins and is taken aback to discover that Alfrida bears a grudge. Later, at her father's funeral, the narrator bumps into a stranger who turns out to be Alfrida's illegitimate daughter, given away at birth and now in touch with her again. The two women go through the anecdote about the dog and the fields and the end of the war yet again. But the daughter's version is significantly different. The narrator is forced to concede some glaring inconsistencies.

The uneasy relationship between fiction and its real-life prototypes is confronted in other Munro stories, notably 'Material' (Munro 1987), and in Raymond Carver's 'Intimacy' (Carver 1998). As any writer knows, most fictional characters are an amalgam, drawn from a number of different sources and transformed by the storytelling process. As John Updike puts it, stories are a kind of rough diamond, 'fragments chipped from experience and rounded by imagination into impersonal artifacts' (Updike 2004: xii). The writer's responsibility is always to their craft. Yet Alfrida's reaction when she recognizes private confidences plundered for public consumption is entirely understandable. The fact that so many of the circumstances have been changed in the fiction-making process only adds insult to injury by distorting the original story.

This is a tricky issue, one which neither Munro nor Carver can resolve. Munro herself has said that she would have found publishing many of her stories impossible if her mother had still been alive. Sometimes it is hard to avoid the feeling that writers are parasitic on other people's lives. 'Family Furnishings' puts the problem in a wider context, showing how we all indulge in the tricks of storytelling from day to day. We all edit our memories and fictionalize the past. The contradictory versions of family history and the long-held secret of Alfrida's pregnancy show how difficult it is, in any case, to establish the unvarnished truth.

The American Tim O'Brien also explores the border between fact and fiction. In 'How to Tell a True War Story', he looks back on soldiers' tales from the Vietnam war, many of them tidying up or dramatizing messy experiences, and some of them attaining a symbolic truth even though, strictly speaking, they are false. 'That's a true story that never happened', he says (O'Brien 1991: 79). What we can take from this and from Munro's story is an understanding that human nature is immensely complex and the drive to make up stories irresistible. As writers our job is not to simplify experience but to leave room for all the inexplicable mysteries we encounter every day.

Autobiographical writing is a good way to grasp those mysteries because memory is naturally disjointed. We retain only partial impressions from the past. Virginia Woolf captures the random quality of these fragments when she describes her very first memory: 'This was of red and purple flowers on a black ground – my mother's dress; and she was sitting either in a train or in an omnibus, and I was on her lap' (Woolf 1976: 64). Was it a train or a bus? It doesn't really matter. It is the red and purple flowers that bring the memory back to life.

Alice Munro has published two story sequences, each linked by a central character – *Lives of Girls and Women* and *The Beggar Maid*. The story sequence or cycle is yet another example of the short story's flexibility as a form. Story cycles are a good way to order autobiographical or biographical material, each individual story moving on to another key theme or turning point in the character's life. Other sequences, such as James Joyce's *Dubliners* and R. K. Narayan's *Malgudi Days* are linked by a real or fictional setting, creating a vibrant, teeming picture of a local neighbourhood. Some of the oldest story cycles are linked by a framing device. Geoffrey Chaucer's *The Canterbury Tales* are narrated by medieval characters on a religious pilgrimage. A few years earlier, the Italian Giovanni Boccaccio published *The Decameron*, narrated by another set of characters who are passing the time while in quarantine during a plague epidemic.

The short-story cycle also has practical advantages for the fiction writer. If you are not in a position to write full time, it is more feasible to complete a series of self-contained stories than to keep trying to pick up the threads in one long continuous narrative. If you are aiming for publication, you can send out the stories individually to magazines while also packaging the whole collection as a novel. *Lives of Girls and Women* is often classified as a novel, along with many other examples, including Jamaica Kincaid's *Annie John*, Irvine Welsh's *Trainspotting*, Amy Tan's *The Joy Luck Club* and David Mitchell's *Ghostwritten*. A first novel is still

REALITY

regarded as more commercially viable than a story collection. Although this is changing, especially in the USA, why not spread your bets? Once you have built up a body of work, look for a central theme, a recurring character, or a location tying your stories together. If you are in a class or a workshop ask your friends or your teachers for advice. They may well have spotted something you are too close to see for yourself.

Activity 1   Observation

Following my advice since Chapter 2, observation should be second nature to you. You should already be keeping your eyes and ears open, on the alert for the stories that surround you. You may find it useful to repeat some of the earlier activities, for instance Activity 2 in Chapter 2, or Activity 5 in Chapter 3. For this activity, return to a public place you visit fairly regularly taking a notebook, and a camera if you wish. You could choose a market, supermarket or a shopping centre; a hospital or old people's home; a school or college; a bus or railway station or an airport. How often have you really noticed what is going on in these places or paid any attention to the people there? In modern society we tend to be wary of strangers, keeping safe in our own little bubble.

Spend at least an hour there. You can do some shopping, catch your bus or go to classes, but you should not be preoccupied by your usual reason for being there. This time you are not rushing through. You are taking your time to look and to listen. Talk to people. Be polite. There is no need to drill the people you meet. It is better just to chat than to bombard them with questions. Think about the time of day. An open market is very different first thing in the morning when the stalls are being set up to the way it is when it is thronged with shoppers; the atmosphere in a hospital ward changes at visiting time.

Describe an incident – real or made up – which typifies that place to you. It can be based on something you have witnessed or something that happened to you, but try writing in the third person, through an omniscient narrator. The incident can be quite small – a lost child, a meeting at the station, a hospital visit. Use dialogue and develop individual characters to bring the incident to life.

Activity 2   Secret lives

Carrying out the previous activity, you should have noticed a whole spectrum of activities. Many of the people whose contributions are essential lead lives that are too often left unsung. Every public place has to be kept clean, for instance, something we take for granted until it fails to happen. The series of stories by the Kenyan Ngũgĩ wa Thiong'o, *Secret Lives*, attempts to redress the balance as a series of character sketches based around the lives of the poorest in his society.

For this exercise, I want you to describe something too often left out of literature – what people do at work. You may have a job of your own, or you can talk to a friend or relation. Annie Proulx's stories in *Close Range* are based on the lives of Wyoming cowboys and ranchers. In all her fiction, Proulx is fascinated by the technical details of specific crafts. The enthusiasm is infectious, but when we read about how to ride rodeo or how to skin a steer, she is also taking us more deeply inside the character. Write a short fictional piece based on a character's experiences at work.

Activity 3   Oral history

As well as drawing on her own experiences, Alice Munro often uses local and family history in her work. Like her fellow Canadian, Alistair MacLeod, she explores the lives of her pioneering forebears who crossed the ocean from Scotland or Ireland to make new lives for themselves. The Chinese American Amy Tan also chronicles the immigrant experience in *The Joy Luck Club*, celebrating the different stories lived by the characters.

If you consider the upheavals of the previous century, you will get some idea of the changes your parents and grandparents have lived through – not just the big events like wars, but social revolutions such as women's liberation, the coming of television and the struggle against racism. Personal accounts bring the past to life in ways the history books can never do. But, as we saw in 'Family Furnishings', the past can be elusive. Memories are unreliable, stories differ and some secrets, for instance a birth out of wedlock, stay buried forever. While there are some facts you may want to establish, the chief interest in these stories lies in the personal details, not in the dry facts and figures.

For this exercise, find a photograph, either from the family album or from a local history source such as a book of old street scenes. You can even use one of yourself, so long as it's at least ten years old. Describe what you see. How did the people in the photo come to be there? If it is a family photo, you will find it useful to talk to family members about their memories of that day and any other people in the picture. Like the characters in 'Family Furnishings' they will be unable to resist telling stories.

Activity 4   News

We have seen several examples of stories inspired by the news – in this chapter, Joyce Carole Oates's 'Where Are You Going, Where Have You Been?' and in Chapter 1, Gala Blau's 'Outfangthief'. Choose a newspaper item on which to base your own fictional story. Like Oates, look for aspects left out of a factual account, such as the inner motivations of the characters involved. Your story does not have to be as grim as these two tales; you can use a more light-hearted story. Feel free to invent characters, change the setting and add other fictional ingredients.

Activity 5   Fifteen

This autobiographical exercise is taken from my chapter on 'Writing the Self' in *The Creative Writing Handbook*. There are several other exercises you might like to try if you are especially interested in personal approaches to writing.

Go back in your mind to when you were roughly fifteen years old. Even if that was only a few years ago it will still seem like a long time ago. Fifteen is a transitional time, between childhood and the beginnings of adult maturity. Make a note of three things from that time – an item of clothing or jewellery, a piece of music and an expression you associate with that time. Nothing dates like a slang expression. Remember Bill and Ted from the movies? *Excellent!* 'Sweet' has replaced 'excellent' as a term of approval, but has no doubt dropped out of fashion by the time you read my words. So far as the music is concerned, there may be a band you followed when you were fifteen, or perhaps you remember a theme tune from television. The clothing or jewellery could anything from a stud you had put in your tongue to a school uniform or sports kit.

Now think about what lies behind these symbols of your fifteen-year-old self. Did you ever get to see the band? What did they mean to you?

Did you have arguments with your parents about getting your tongue pierced? When did you use that expression? Who else used it? Who was your best friend and where are they now? Write a brief account (under 1000 words) of something that happened when you were around that age. Don't worry if you aren't quite sure whether you were exactly fifteen, or if some details are hazy.

First of all trying writing your account in the past tense. Then write it again in the present tense. Which do you prefer? Which do you feel brings you closest to the original experience?

Activity 6   Absent friends

The previous activity may have already started you thinking about old friends. This exercise centres on a real-life person – a friend, a relation or just an acquaintance. You may have known them well or only slightly but, for whatever reason, nowadays you see them rarely or never. The aim here is to experiment with ellipsis and shifting time frames mapping out the sort of structure Munro uses in 'Family Furnishings'.

Rough out your first memories of that person. Once again, don't worry if not all the details are there, or if you're not quite sure which was the first time. Just describe what you have got as clearly and specifically as you can. What do you associate with that particular person? Munro mentions Alfrida's large, irregular teeth which are later replaced by false ones. Once you have the first occasion, make similar notes on the last time you had contact with them. If you can remember their words, write down what they said. This is a very approximate record.

You now have two islands in time, made from these sets of impressions. How are you going to make a bridge between them? Try filling in with describing your life in the intervening days, months or years. Remember not to get bogged down in background information. Focus on a succession of key moments and important images. As you work these rough notes into a first draft, experiment again with tense. You can also try reordering these moments, starting with the 'ending' and then flashing back to the first memory.

Activity 7   Moment of decision

Remember a time when you made some sort of decision – an important choice, such as the end of a relationship, or a relatively trivial one, such as growing a beard. Quickly write down everything you can remember about that moment. We are less interested in analysing the reasons behind the decision than in what it felt like within that moment. Where were you? What finally tipped the balance?

You are now going to change this autobiographical account into fiction. Graham Greene advised turning your life into fiction by changing one significant detail. Take this advice. Don't just change the names. Change the sex of your protagonist, or move the story to another setting. You will find that one relatively small change generates others, adding new fictional dimensions to your tale.

When you are turning experiences into fiction, be careful not lose the specifics. Alice Munro gives her towns fictional names but they are definitely in south-western Ontario. They are not anonymous, colourless, nowhere-in-particular places. As we have seen in this chapter, stories grow in the telling. Redrafting the activities you have completed this time, you will find them drifting away from their origins and taking on lives of their own.

7

Love, sex and shaping a story

Sex, love and romance

Like comic fiction, which I discussed in Chapter 3, romantic and erotic writing surfaces in every type of genre. Annie Proulx's 'Brokeback Mountain' is a love story between two cowboys, combining a realist account of life on the range with a doomed homosexual romance. William Gibson's 'New Rose Hotel' (in *Burning Chrome*) is an elegy for a lost cyberlover. We have already seen how Angela Carter brings out the eroticism underlying the traditional folk tale in 'The Company of Wolves' (Chapter 4). The three core examples in this chapter achieve widely varying effects through romantic or erotic subject matter. 'Death Constant Beyond Love' by the Colombian Gabriel García Márquez is a tightly compressed narrative evoking intense physical desire through sensual description. Chekhov's 'Lady with Lapdog' takes a wryly comic approach to an adulterous affair which has surprising consequences. The contemporary American writer Rebecca Brown subverts conventional romantic symbolism in her lesbian revenge fantasy, 'Dr Frankenstein, I Presume'.

As a concentrated form, the short story is very good at expressing the intensity of sexual desire. Though none of these stories are sexually explicit, they all create an emotional response in the reader. In recent years, unashamedly erotic fiction has become more respectable, especially for women, with anthologies such as the Black Lace *Wicked Words* series becoming increasingly popular. In July 2004, Anaïs Nin's erotic classic

Delta of Venus was the best-selling short-story collection in the UK. *Sexy Shorts for Summer* from the small publishing house Accent Press is also in the top ten. The boom has expanded into niche markets, for lesbians and gays, black people, South-East Asians and other ethnic groups. The Internet magazine, *Nerve*, describes itself as 'a fearless intelligent forum for both genders ... Nerve intends to be more graphic, forthright, and topical than "erotica", but less blockheadedly masculine than "pornography".' Supported by established writers including Mary Gaitskell and Alice Sebold, *Nerve* sets itself high artistic standards and, with a print edition in the pipeline, already belongs to the mainstream.

If you want to enter this specialized market, you must enjoy reading erotica, or your writing will lack conviction. You will need to pay as much attention to plot development, characterization and setting as in any other genre. The sex must take place between consenting adults. Reputable publishers are not interested in extreme graphic violence, incest or under-age sex. They want you to be naughty, not nasty. Although Anaïs Nin is able to tackle taboo areas in *Delta of Venus*, this is because her work is now considered to be a twentieth-century classic. *Nerve*'s submission guidelines are generally applicable: 'Here is what we do not publish: porn, "erotica", play-by-play sexploits and purple fiction (read: overwrought romances in the airport-novel genre). Nerve aims to be frank about sex, but not necessarily explicit' (www.nerve.com).

Despite the publishers' disavowals, *Nerve* does contain explicit material, and if you have moral objections, you had better avoid their web site. The guidelines are most clear about what they do not want, which is basically anything formulaic or clichéd. The challenge is to find fresh new ways to write about sex.

However, this chapter is mostly concerned with writing about love. Love stories have a universal appeal. Everyone, no matter how cynical, knows how it feels to become obsessed by another person, to plan a first date, to suffer unrequited love or to endure the end of the affair. A love affair also provides the perfect dramatic structure for a short story. Here we might turn to Chekhov, who always advised keeping it simple. He said, 'The centre of gravity should be in two persons: him and her' (Chekhov 1994: 33). Once you have a sexual tension between 'him and her' (or 'her and her' or 'him and him') the narrative starts to unroll. Later in this chapter, I will be looking in more detail at how character and plot develop, using the idea of a love story as a narrative framework.

There will be more advice on writing about sex and love; and, since this is the final chapter, the activities will conclude with suggestions for editing and redrafting your work.

Desire: 'Death Constant Beyond Love' (Gabriel García Márquez, 1972)

Gabriel García Márquez is one of the foremost 'magic realist' writers in South America, though he has often said that he does not invent the fantastic and mythical elements in his stories. His work draws on folklore and oral tradition to generate vividly dramatic tales of life in small towns and peasant communities. 'Death Constant Beyond Love' is no exception. The opening sentence grabs the attention immediately: 'Senator Onésimo Sánchez had six months and eleven days to go before his death when he found the woman of his life' (Márquez 1991: 219).

The title already subverts expectations, reversing the standard cliché. This first sentence foreshadows the ending before the story has even begun. Márquez builds up suspense by creating anticipation. His story is very brief at less than 1800 words; by compressing the narrative he emphasizes the violent impact of physical attraction. Sánchez meets Laura Farina on the campaign trail. He has stopped at her dead-end village along with his carnival retinue of performing Indians, fireworks and musicians. Márquez satisfies our curiosity by telling us that the senator has already been told of his terminal illness. This secret knowledge subverts the phoney optimism in his electoral address:

'We are here for the purpose of defeating nature,' he began, against all his convictions. 'We will no longer be foundlings in our own country, orphans of God in a realm of thirst and bad climate, exiles in our own land. We will be a different people, ladies and gentlemen, we will be a great and happy people.'
There was a pattern to his circus. As he spoke his aide threw clusters of paper birds into the air and the artificial creatures took on life, flew about the platform of planks, and went out to sea.
(Márquez 1991: 221)

The Senator promises 'rainmaking machines, portable breeders for table animals, the oils of happiness which would make vegetables grow in the saltpeter and clumps of pansies in the window boxes' (Márquez 1991: 221).

Laura is the beautiful daughter of Nelson Farina, a convicted murderer who escaped from Devil's Island and has spent the past twelve years petitioning the Senator for a false identity card. Márquez prolongs the suspense by delaying their meeting until halfway through the story, lingering on his description of the Senator's farcical visit. Sánchez encounters Laura by chance on his customary walkabout: 'She was wearing a cheap, faded Guajiro Indian robe, her head was decorated with colored bows, and her face was painted as protection against the sun, but even in that state of disrepair it was possible to imagine that there had never been another so beautiful in the whole world' (Márquez 1991: 223).

Márquez constantly uses hyperbole – exaggeration or overstatement – to evoke Laura's extreme beauty and Sánchez's state of arousal. Later he says her skin has 'the same color and the same solar density as crude oil, her hair was the mane of a young mare, and her huge eyes were brighter than the light' (Márquez 1991: 225).

These hyperbolic and magical elements contribute to the story's hallucinatory qualities. When Farina sends his daughter to petition the Senator later that evening, she is mesmerized by a paper butterfly he has fashioned from a calendar, and then by thousands of bank notes floating in his room. There is a rational explanation; they are carried by air from an electrical fan. Yet the seediness and corruption of the setting is momentarily transformed by Laura's presence. The rose Sánchez uses in his buttonhole, keeping it alive in a glass of water, is a small miracle in this desert region. Again Márquez undercuts his own fairy-tale imagery. Laura is unfazed: she has heard about roses already. Márquez reins in the story's romanticism before it mutates into sentimentality.

Márquez delays this second, full encounter until the story's closing stages. If we want to draw the analogy, we could say that he has skilfully prolonged the narrative foreplay, intensifying the eventual climax. He slows down the pace at this point. Earlier sections have been largely summarized, with very little dialogue. The exchange between Sánchez and Laura is the only conversation in the story. In comparison with the densely packed descriptive passages that have come before, the narrative is much simpler and more direct. Márquez keeps the reader's attention by carefully pacing the narrative and varying its texture with different types of discourse.

With nothing to lose, the dying man undresses. The physical details are carefully described, evoking scent and texture:

Just to have some time to think, he held Laura Farina tightly between his knees, embraced her about the waist, and lay down on his back on the cot. Then he realized that she was naked under her dress, for her body gave off the dark fragrance of an animal of the woods, but her heart was frightened and her skin disturbed by a glacial sweat.

'No one loves us,' he sighed.

Laura Farina tried to say something, but there was only enough air for her to breathe. He laid her down beside him to help her, he put out the light and the room was in the shadow of the rose.

(Márquez 1991: 226)

The sensuous description carries the reader along until once again, Márquez punctures the effect he has so lovingly sustained:

The senator caressed her slowly, seeking her with his hand, barely touching her, but where he expected to find her, he came across something iron that was in the way.

'What have you got there?'

'A padlock,' she said.

(Márquez 1991: 226)

It's a set up. Laura's father will supply the key when he gets his identity card. Many readers will feel uneasy about Laura's passivity in this situation and the animal imagery connected to her. Yet the closing paragraphs are deeply moving. The Senator tells her to forget about the key. He just wants to sleep with her:

The senator held her about the waist, sank his face into woods-animal armpit, and gave in to terror. Six months and eleven days later he would die in that same position, debased and repudiated because of the public scandal with Laura Farina and weeping with rage at dying without her.

(Márquez 1991: 227)

Laura's head is resting on his shoulder; both characters are alone and finding comfort in each other. The association between sex and death is common in art and literature across the ages. The French term for orgasm is *petit mort* or 'little death'. Temporarily, at least, we are annihilated by physical pleasure.

More pragmatically, in representations of intense desire there is nowhere else to go but death. If Romeo and Juliet had survived, moved in together and raised a family, they would no longer be romantic figures. You can't stay forever in the throes of an all-consuming passion; a relationship may deepen, but after a time you lose that initial obsession. Obsessive love does not belong in the real world; and Márquez's story is not strictly speaking 'realistic', despite its oblique comments on political corruption in his own country.

Eroticism depends on fantasy. Like Carter in 'The Company of Wolves', Márquez transports us to an imaginary playground – a very unusual playground, in that it is both pleasurable and, at times, disturbing. The exotic imagery – the paper birds and butterflies and the shadow of the rose – all contribute to the heightened atmosphere. Everything is in excess, including the extreme desert heat. High temperatures are often associated with feverish eroticism. In the much more understated 'Lady with Lapdog', the couple first make love in a stifling hotel room, perfumed with the Japanese scents the lady has brought back from her shopping.

As we have seen, the erotic charge in 'Death Constant Beyond Love' is also delivered by a tightly controlled narrative pace. Márquez's sensuous prose carries the reader along; and when Sánchez and Laura are finally alone, the language is evocative, rather than fully explicit. The tenderness of the closing images achieves a more profound eroticism than a fully consummated sexual act. Eroticism thrives on what is hidden or just glimpsed – the Senator 'barely touching' Laura in the darkness.

Sánchez and Laura make unlikely lovers. He is well-to-do, has been educated abroad, a family man with five children. Only the desperate circumstances of his illness propel him towards his strange destiny. Laura is treated as little more than a chattel, raised by her disreputable father. By pairing such contrasting lovers, writers are able to explore the chemistry between them. They may even seem incompatible. In love stories, plot is often generated by the obstacles in the way of the lovers' union. Seeming incompatibility can function in this way. But very often the obstacle is marriage to somebody else. Adultery is a staple ingredient in the love story, and this is the subject of Chekhov's 'Lady with Lapdog'.

Adultery: 'Lady with Lapdog' (Anton Chekhov, 1899)

In contrast with the heightened atmosphere of the previous story, 'Lady with Lapdog' is an everyday tale in a realistic setting, examining the psychology of sexual desire at greater leisure. (It is four times longer than 'Death Constant Beyond Love'.) The story unfolds in a Russian holiday resort from Chekhov's time, just over 100 years ago. At first glance, its structure seems meandering and anecdotal. Yet Chekhov controls narrative pace just as firmly as Márquez, and includes nothing that is unnecessary. Chekhov said that he always cut the first and last paragraph. In keeping with this advice, the narrative opens abruptly, telling us about the lady without further delay: 'The appearance on the front of a new arrival – a lady with a lapdog – became the topic of general conversation' (Chekhov 1971: 264).

He sketches in her appearance quickly; she is 'fair, not very tall' (Chekhov 1971: 264), and wears a small hat. While Márquez's Laura was stunningly beautiful, Chekhov's heroine remains non-descript. The only thing that really marks her out is the little white Pomeranian that follows in her wake.

The lady in the description is seen from the viewpoint of Chekhov's other main character, Dmitry Dmitrich Gurov. We are given much more information about him than we have learnt about her:

> He was not yet forty, but he had a twelve-year-old daughter and two schoolboy sons. He had been married off when he was still in his second year at university, and his wife seemed to him now to be almost twice his age. She was a tall, black-browed woman, erect, dignified, austere, and, as she liked to describe herself, a 'thinking person'. She was a great reader, preferred the new 'advanced' spelling, called her husband by the more formal 'Dimitry' and not the familiar 'Dmitry'; and though he secretly considered her not particularly intelligent, narrow-minded, and inelegant, he was afraid of her and disliked being at home. He had been unfaithful to her for a long time, he was often unfaithful to her, and that was why, perhaps, he almost always spoke ill of women, and when men discussed women in his presence, he described them as *the lower breed*.
> (Chekhov 1971: 264)

Interestingly, we are learning about Gurov through a description of somebody else – his wife back in Moscow. As Chekhov confirms, he is a slippery customer, hard to pin down. Despite his apparent disdain for the female sex he is more at ease with women than he is with men: 'There was something attractive, something elusive in his appearance, in his character and his whole person, that women found interesting and irresistible; he was aware of it, and was himself drawn to them by some irresistible force' (Chekhov 1971: 265).

Psychologically the portrait is very acute. Gurov is a complex, contradictory person, not a particularly good man, but a fine example of a 'round' fictional character, who can change and develop during the course of the narrative. It so happens that Chekhov was himself a womanizer. The only way we can really get inside the skin of our characters is by borrowing from our own experiences and watching real people in action.

The plot develops through casual encounters. He gets talking to her in a restaurant, but does not see her again for a week. Almost automatically they become lovers. In Anna's hotel room, Gurov compares his new mistress with his former conquests:

> From his past he preserved the memory of carefree, good-natured women, whom love had made gay and who were grateful to him for the happiness he gave them, however short-lived; and of women like his wife, who made love without sincerity, with unnecessary talk, affectedly, hysterically, with such an expression, as though it were not love or passion, but something much more significant; and of two or three very beautiful, frigid women, whose faces suddenly lit up with a predatory expression, an obstinate desire to take, to snatch from life more than it could give [. . .]
>
> (Chekhov 1971: 268)

This is a very revealing passage, in terms of both male and female sexuality. Like Maupassant, whose work I discussed in the previous chapter, Chekhov maintains a detached, non-judgemental style. But he probes much more deeply into the motivations behind his characters' actions. Often these are difficult to establish. Anna is overcome with guilt yet she continues the affair. Gurov is hardly the first man to have said to a weeping woman 'I don't understand [. . .] what it is you want' (Chekhov 1971: 269).

One meeting follows another as her husband's arrival is delayed. The narrative is loosely structured, one passage following another seemingly at random as their days together blend into a kind of dream. These stretches of narrative, where nothing much seems to be happening, are essential to plot development, especially in longer stories. Chekhov uses natural imagery to create mood and atmosphere, subtly reflecting the tensions building up beneath the surface: 'Later, when they went out, there was not a soul on the promenade, the town with its cypresses looked quite dead, but the sea was still roaring and dashing itself against the shore; a single launch tossed on the waves, its lamps flickering sleepily' (Chekhov 1971: 270). Fiction entails conflict and change, but these changes emerge gradually. These quieter, reflective passages suggest the passage of time, preparing the reader for turning points in the narrative. Storytelling has its own rhythms. Like an orchestral piece, a short story consists of different movements, operating at an ever-changing pace.

Suddenly Anna's husband cancels his holiday and she returns home. It was fun, but now it's over. Yet, home in Moscow, Gurov cannot forget her: 'In the evenings she gazed at him from the bookcase, from the fireplace, from the corner – he heard her breathing, the sweet rustle of her dress. In the street he followed women with his eyes, looking for anyone who resembled her' (Chekhov 1971: 273).

Yet another reason why short fiction is so suited to love stories is its ability to evoke loss and absence. Slipping easily between past and present, it is able to summon back fleeting memories based on sense impressions. Compare this passage with another by the contemporary American writer Nell Freudenberger. The narrator remembers the nightwatchman passing by as she conducted her illicit love affair:

> It was six o'clock, and I recognized the whiskey-colored light on the white sheets: Arun pinning my wrists down with his hands, holding me tight beneath him so I couldn't move. It was not like with other people; he took it seriously, as if these were necessary things we were doing. Those evenings – Arun's car in front of the house, everyone knowing we were there – the whole world was in our room; tiny inscrutable figures moving in a pattern across our sheets.
>
> (Freudenberger 2003: 26)

Arun is now dead; but his presence is as real as Anna's ghostly breath in Gurov's study.

Finally Gurov sets off, with no clear purpose, for Anna's home town. The tension builds as he tracks down her address and hangs around outside her house. Could that be Anna he can hear playing the piano? A white Pomeranian comes out of the house, but he is so nervous he forgets the dog's name. The frustrations pile up. Stuck in a dreary town in pursuit of this ordinary woman, he is furious with himself. The effect is comic, but also rather touching. The agony is prolonged still further when he pursues Anna and her husband to the theatre. He makes himself known to her during the interval. Anna is dumb with amazement. Chekhov choreographs the scene in breathless detail:

> She looked up at him and turned pale, then looked at him again in panic, unable to believe her eyes, clenching her fan and lorgnette in her hand and apparently trying hard not to fall into a dead faint. Both were silent. She sat and he stood, frightened by her embarrassment and not daring to sit down beside her.
>
> (Chekhov 1971: 277)

This frantic rush of words – Chekhov goes on to describe the orchestra tuning up and the lovers scuttling onto the stairs – accelerates like a racecourse commentary gathering speed as the horses surge towards the finishing line. When the lovers are at last able to speak, broken syntax and repeated phrases maintain this urgency: 'I've been thinking of you all the time. The thought of you kept me alive. And yet I tried to hard to forget you – why, oh why did you come?' (Chekhov 1971: 277).

This is the climactic scene of the story. Like Márquez, Chekhov foregrounds a decisive moment through dialogue between the lovers. After the relentless speed of this hasty meeting, the narrative settles into its previous leisurely pace. Anna and Gurov resume their affair. Every few months she comes to Moscow, on the rather ironic pretext that she is seeing her gynaecologist. Then in another sudden shift, like the change in direction when Anna went home from her holiday, Gurov spots his grey hairs in the mirror. His looks are fading. He reflects on the women who thought they loved him for what they imagined was there, and realizes that in all this time he has only loved once. It is ludicrous that he and Anna should hide their love.

The story ends inconclusively. It leaves Anna and Gurov discussing their options. These would be very limited at that time, when divorce or extramarital relationships were, in general, frowned upon. But the open ending lifts the mood because it is dynamic. It anticipates the future:

> And it seemed to them that in only a few more minutes a solution would be found and a new, beautiful life would begin; but both of them knew very well that the end was still a long, long way away and that the most complicated and difficult part was only just beginning.
>
> (Chekhov 1971: 281)

The obvious obstacles to the lovers in 'Lady with Lapdog' are their mutual spouses. But the other obstacle to happiness lies in human perversity. Gurov's pride will not let him admit his love for Anna until the end of the story. Anna's love increases despite her guilty conscience. The characters' persistence in punishing themselves develops the plot further. In both 'Lady with Lapdog' and 'Death Constant Beyond Love', the hero finds his true love late in life, as he becomes conscious of his mortality. Both men are willing to stake everything on this last chance before time runs out. For both writers, love is inexplicable, a sudden miracle descending on those who least expect it.

Looking back over the story, we can see how Chekhov has structured the narrative as a whole, sustaining tension by varying the pace. Slow interludes are punctured by the unexpected. The holiday romance is curtailed by a letter calling Anna home. With Gurov back in Moscow, events reach another hiatus until his sudden impulse to track her down again. Periods of stasis, where narrative developments are re-enforced rather than driving forwards, alternate with faster-paced passages introducing drastic change. The turning points are based on actions – an external intervention, such as a letter; or the character's initiative – Gurov's active decision. This broad pattern is repeated on a smaller scale, for instance in the long delay between Gurov's arrival in Anna's home town and the confrontation at the theatre. When the affair is re-established towards the end of the story, we reach another narrative impasse, with the lovers perpetuating their double lives indefinitely. As we have seen, the status quo is again shattered, though this time the change is more internal and psychological, and is not associated with clear-cut decisions or dramatic interventions.

The pace may be quickened when the narrative shifts forward abruptly, summarizing events. This happens when Anna leaves, after receiving her husband's letter:

> She took a carriage to the railway station, and he saw her off. The drive took a whole day. When she got into the express train, after the second bell, she said:
>
> 'Let me have another look at you . . . One last look. So.'
>
> She did not cry, but looked sad, just as if she were ill, and her face quivered.
>
> (Chekhov 1971: 271)

Writers are always being urged to 'show not tell', but it's a little more complicated. The trick is knowing when to show and when to tell. Chekhov *tells* us how long the drive took; he *shows* us the scene at the station. As in the later scene at the theatre, he highlights the characters' inner turmoil through snatches of dialogue and small descriptive details – for instance, the look on Anna's face, which is seen through Gurov's eyes.

I use the word 'scene' deliberately. One way of approaching structure and pace is to imagine your story as scenes in a film. Chekhov 'cuts' from the letter to the journey to the station to the last farewell. In your own fiction, consider how it would move from scene to scene; which are the big moments – decisive actions and emotional turning points, moments of crisis, conflict or confrontation? Paradoxically, the pace quickens when you linger on these highly charged moments, taking the reader deep inside their emotional core. You need to take the time to exploit them fully. Pace is also affected by syntax. It quickens when sentences and paragraphs are short or fragmented. Chekhov describes the parting in clipped, almost flat sentences.

I have stressed the intensity of the 'big scenes' in the narrative, but you should remember this doesn't necessarily mean spelling out your characters' responses. Although Chekhov goes on to analyse Gurov's mental state at some length, as he stands alone on the platform, the description is restrained. Often new writers try to convey emotions by giving their characters a severe case of collywobbles – churning stomachs, knees like jelly and other physiological symptoms. When Chekhov says 'Gurov listened to the churring of the grasshoppers and the humming of the telegraph wires with a feeling as though he had just woken up' (Chekhov 1971: 272) he relies on understatement, using the character's perceptions of the external world to suggest his internal state of mind.

There will be more on structure and pace in Activities 7 and 8, which close this chapter. Structure, pace and narrative voice are all intertwined.

If you look back at my discussion of comic timing in Chapter 3, you can see this is also related to pace. The comic anecdote, perfected by Mark Twain and Garrison Keillor, may appear to be meandering and off the cuff, but it is much more than spontaneous rambling. Within any type of story, pace may slow or quicken, but the narrative should never drag. Sometimes, reading a lengthy novel, I know I can skip a page or two without losing anything. The writer couldn't get away with that in a short story where every word counts. Cutting out the dead weight – redundant words, sentences, passages – should be one of your priorities as you redraft. Reading your work aloud to yourself helps you find the rhythmic pace to 'orchestrate' a narrative, alongside other aspects of the editing process.

Revenge: 'Dr Frankenstein, I Presume' (Rebecca Brown, 1989)

Revenge is the high-octane fuel powering many a narrative engine. It crops up frequently in crime fiction, for instance in Ruth Rendell's 'A Dark Blue Perfume', where, in retirement, a divorced husband broods on his past wrongs with tragic consequences. Other writers, notably Roald Dahl, are inclined to take a more comic view of murderous spouses. No one harbours a grudge like a lover spurned, betrayed or jealous; and the idea of revenge is very tempting. The British woman who cut her husband's expensive suits to shreds became a sort of folk heroine. Writing or reading about revenge gives a vicarious satisfaction. However fraught your life may be you have one consolation: as a writer, you will always have the last word.

In Rebecca Brown's 'Dr Frankenstein, I Presume' the first-person, present-tense narrative has the fluidity of a dream. Using a present-tense narrative adds immediacy and urgency to a story which starts even more precipitately than 'Lady with Lapdog':

> I am in my bed and almost out, and almost where I can forget. But just when I'm about to fall, my loyal dark assistant is beside my bed. She shakes me awake. I see her masked face, pale as a moon. Her mouth moves underneath her mask. 'Doctor,' she rasps, 'There's going to be a storm.'
>
> (Brown 1989: 1)

Brown parodies the conventions of the *Frankenstein* movie as her narrator, still in pyjamas, takes a cab to a Gothic castle, complete with bats. But these are intermingled with borrowings from hospital drama – swinging doors, steel scalpels, a surgeon's gown and gloves. Our narrator has 'various diplomas from UCLA and Transylvania State' (Brown 1989: 3).

Present-tense narrative is very closely allied to narrative in film. Brown continues in parodic mode by using film language:

> Cut to bright silver lamp hanging from slick beige modern ceiling. Roll into it. Fuzz focus to white. Fade into crisp white sheet. Pull back to show the white sheet on the rickety bed raised up towards the skylight. Close-up of thick, cracked leather straps with huge metal buckles. Pan the sheet beneath whose contours lie –
>
> Did I forget to mention whose the body was? How could I? When there was only one, and only ever has been one, on whom I would be qualified to operate.
>
> (Brown 1989: 3)

Brown is using humour to tackle the pain of betrayal. Sitting alone feeling miserable does not make much of a story. Fantasy energizes a passive experience, turning it into action. The first-person, present-tense narrative, addressed to the unnamed 'you', heightens the emotional intensity. Like Márquez, Brown builds sensuality into the vivid imagery and the textures of the language: 'Your white back arcing in the dark. Your dark mouth open like a pool' (Brown 1989: 3). The repetitions and sound patterns ('arc'/'dark') are close to poetry, often allied with the short-story form by practitioners and critics.

Brown sustains the *Frankenstein | Dr Kildare* parody, as the narrator sets about the operation to open up her lover's body and extract the heart. The heart is, of course, another poetic device, symbol of love and devotion, now become a Valentine's Day cliché. In 'How I Finally Lost My Heart', the British writer Doris Lessing subverts the image by taking her title literally: 'a heart raw and bleeding and fresh from one's side is not the prettiest sight' (Park and Heaton 1992: 167). But the heart in Brown's story is made of candy with red lettering. Its colour keeps changing with the words: '*Trust Me, Kiss Me, You Belong to Me, You're Mine*' (Brown 1989: 5). The story becomes a diatribe against the treacherous lover: 'the most you've ever been is less than human, sub-alive, a bloodless, heartless, pretty-faced cadaver' (Brown 1989: 5) This is the kind of put-down we always wish we'd thought of at the time.

Brown's narrator goes one better than that, acting out the literal implications of the phrase. We identify with the narrator much more in this fantasy enactment than we might do in a realistic rendition of her bitterness and resentment – common human failings, but still not particularly appealing to the reader.

Part-way through the operation, the patient revives. Mesmerized by the sight of her pretty brown eyes, the narrator keeps her grip on the heart stuck fast in her lover's chest. Once again, a writer uses the exchange of dialogue to highlight a critical moment. She builds up the suspense with carefully staged pauses:

> 'Don't you feel this?' I mash my hands together hard.
> There is a pause.
> 'What?' You're petulant. 'I don't feel a thing.'
> 'Keep your eyes closed,' I say. 'Tell me when you feel something.'
> I clench my hands around your slippery heart. I take a deep breath
> then rip your heart out of you.
>
> (Brown 1989: 6–7)

But the lover still feels nothing. She lies on the operating table, oblivious and sleepily seductive. The narrator is paralysed. We leave her poised in mid-decision, unable to take her eyes off the woman who betrayed her. It is not quite a revenge story after all. But it has been quite a ride.

Recognition

Within the framework of a love story you can do almost anything. In John Updike's 'The Persistence of Desire', a married man bumps into an old flame on a visit back home. Updike's comic observations mingle with eroticism. Sitting bored in an ophthalmologist's waiting room, Clyde glances at a magazine which informs him: 'Science reveals that the cells of the normal human body are replaced *in toto* every seven years' (Updike 2004: 81). Still waiting, he gazes nostalgically through the window. Then someone comes through the door: 'When he saw who it was, although every cell in his body had been replaced since he had last seen her, his hands jerked in his lap and blood bounded against his skin' (Updike 2004: 82).

Like the lady with the lapdog, the object of Clyde's desire is unexceptional. It is the ordinary things about Janet that appeal to him, attributes that would not normally be considered attractive. He is drawn to 'an unsleeping tranquillity marked by that pretty little lavender puffiness below the eyes' (Updike 2004: 82). He does not mind her chubbiness now. Updike milks further humour from the situation when Clyde's sight is blurred by eyedrops. He is determined to seduce Janet, but can hardly see where he is going, either literally or figuratively.

In Chapter 2, I spoke about the 'epiphany', the moment of illumination, which provides the turning point in image-based fiction. Gurov's sudden self-knowledge when he sees his grey hair in the mirror could be seen as an epiphanic moment. But this sense of recognition also extends to the reader, when fiction helps us see familiar experiences through fresh eyes.

'Lovers' by the British writer Rebecca Ray is an understated account of what happens when a young woman decides to move in with her boyfriend. Ray simply describes the practicalities of packing and moving, alluding now and then to the woman's sadness at leaving her parents:

> Now, she didn't want to leave. She thought about telling them that she was tired now and she might stay another night. But she was picking up her boyfriend at six thirty. He'd have his stuff all stacked up by the porch and he'd be waiting for her; he'd have that smile.
>
> (Blincoe and Thorne 2001: 195)

By not naming her characters, Ray implies they could be anyone. There is no background information and no specific setting. This could risk making the story vague and colourless, but the attention to movement and gesture compensates for the characters' anonymity:

> She opened the door for them.
> Once they were inside, though, her mother said only good things. She walked around and touched the cupboards and opened them, she looked at the window fastenings and moved the table a little bit, looking underneath at its legs. She touched almost everything in the flat but she only said good things.
>
> (Blincoe and Thorne 2001: 192)

When you begin a piece of fiction, your first aim is plain and simple – to tell a good story. As 'Lovers' shows, the most basic of plots and the most ordinary situation can be transformed into a compelling story. Even the seemingly 'plotless' stories we examined in Chapter 2 contain the potential for conflict and suspense. In James Kelman's 'Not Not While the Giro', this is enacted within the character rather than externally. In Alice Munro's 'Family Furnishings', it derives largely from the narrative puzzles intriguing the reader. Who was Alfrida really? And do memories deceive? As Angela Carter said, the writer poses questions without answers.

A good story makes the reader curious. They have no choice; they have to read on. To write that story, you should be curious yourself. In Chapter 1, I quoted Stephen King who said that stories are 'found things, like fossils in the ground' (King 2001: 188). His expression echoes an archaeological metaphor used by Katherine Anne Porter: 'My work is done at a subterranean level and fragments of work come to the surface. I record them as they come up' (Givner 1983: 203). Both writers stress the buried, unconscious forces shaping the words on the page. Whatever type of story you write, your goal is to recognize these strange artefacts and to explore them without trying too hard to force a meaning or to make them fit your preconceptions.

In this final chapter, I have paid special attention to structure and pace. But the structure arises from the tale you have to tell. You may sometimes start writing because you want to experiment with a particular structure, but more often than not the structure evolves with the material. Structure does not dictate content. Concepts you may come across in other writing manuals – 'the hero's journey', 'story arc' and suchlike – can help you through the later stages but your early drafts are best improvised. Like love itself, stories appear where you least expect them, and in every shape and form. So be ready for surprises – for yourself and for the reader.

Activity 1   Sexy

Spend ten minutes writing down everything that comes into your head when you read that word 'sexy'. This is one of those exercises that you need to do as quickly as your pen can move across the paper. Don't think. Don't analyse. You can be as frank or as silly as you like. No one's going to read it. Write down what (or who) makes you feel sexy; you can also add associations, pleasant or unpleasant.

This short exercise is designed to make you think about how to describe sex or write erotically. Of course, you don't have to describe sex at all. In 'Lady with Lapdog', Chekhov throws a discreet veil over what happens between the kiss and the walk on the promenade. 'Later', he says, 'when they went out' (Chekhov 1971: 270), like many writers before and since using 'later' to signal ellipsis. Sex is notoriously difficult to describe, which is why the British *Literary Review* bestows an annual Bad Sex Award on hapless novelists deemed to have failed in the attempt.

Look at what you have just written. Some images and phrases that are not overtly sexual might still form the basis for erotic writing. If you have been fairly explicit, how difficult was it to find the right words? One of the reasons why writing about sex is so tricky is that people tend to approach it differently to any other activity. The passages cited for the Bad Sex Award often seemed to have been produced in a vacuum, disconnected from the rest of the novel. The characters' sexual acrobatics are recounted in gruelling detail, as if they had nothing to do with their normal thoughts and activities. There is also a problem with vocabulary. The prose sounds either like something from a medical textbook or from the 'blockheaded' pornography derided by *Nerve*. It is best to stick to simple, down-to-earth language, using the terms that are natural to your own speech, and to your characters.

The exercise may also have thrown out some more ambiguous responses to the word. In 'Sexy', by the American-based Jhumpa Lahiri, Miranda, who is having an affair with a married man, asks a child what he means when he says the word 'sexy'. He tells her, 'It means loving someone you don't know' (Lahiri 2000: 107). Earlier in the story, Miranda was flattered when her lover called her 'sexy'; now she is not so sure.

Activity 2   Love letters

Write a fictional love letter (snail mail or e-mail). The character is either declaring their love or telling the recipient how much they miss them. Remember the purpose of such a letter is to communicate affection and desire. How that is expressed will depend on your character. Some people are effusive, using endearments and even pet names. Other people have a roundabout way of showing their love.

This exercise continues the work in the previous exercise, exploring ways of suggesting eroticism and romance. You may use humour if you wish, or give your letter-writer hidden, perhaps sinister, intentions. Incorporating letters into a short story is a useful method for introducing the first person into a predominantly third-person narrative. Alice Munro often adopts this approach. The title story of *Hateship, Friendship, Courtship, Loveship, Marriage* (2001) revolves around a love letter sent as a joke. 'A Wilderness Station' (Munro 1995) is told entirely through a series of letters and memoirs.

Activity 3   The end of the affair

As we have seen, a confrontation between the lovers, using dialogue, often serves as a dramatic climax. To practise your skills in dialogue, describe a scene between a couple in which one is trying to break up with the other. They may struggle to get the words out or perhaps their partner misunderstands or deliberately ignores what they are being told. Or they may hurl abuse at each other. You may wish to consult the activities on dialogue in Chapter 3. There must be some speech, but you should also include description. There is no need for background information at this stage.

Activity 4   First love

Did you ever have a crush on someone when you were very young? In 'Miriam', by the Czech writer Ivan Klíma, the narrator queues for milk during the German occupation of the Second World War. He is served by a girl who keeps smiling at him and unaccountably giving him extra rations. Smitten, he practises what he is going to say to her, but before he can pluck up the courage to ask her out she suddenly, and apparently just as inexplicably, starts ignoring him. Describe your own 'first love'.

Activity 5   Eternal triangle

Two's company, three's a crowd. There are endless variations on the 'eternal triangle' – and not just the ones involving unfaithful husbands, wives and lovers. What about characters who are torn between hanging round with their pals or seeing their new girlfriend/boyfriend? In Raymond Carver's 'Boxes', the protagonist's new relationship seems blighted by his mother. But what about children who make life hell for their new stepmother or their new dad? Write three monologues, describing each character's account of their particular 'triangle'.

Activity 6   Genre bending

Contemporary short fiction often mingles different genres. Ramsey Campbell's *Scared Stiff* collection and the two *Love in Vein* anthologies edited by Poppy Z. Brite combine horror stories with the erotic. Create your own generic hybrid. Match the erotic, the romantic or a love story with another genre discussed in this book, or another of your own choosing. You may use parody if you wish. This is your chance to let your imagination run riot. How about a love story between robots? Or an erotic ghost story?

Activity 7   Him/her

This is an extended exercise in plot development and characterization, using Chekhov's 'him and her', the narrative's 'centre of gravity'. You are aiming to produce a complete short story. It must be some kind of a love story, but within that framework it can be comic or tragic, realistic or fantastic – anything you like, so long as the relationship develops in the course of the narrative. You may use ideas from the previous six exercises.

Stage 1

First of all, spend five minutes making notes on your two lovers. If you have a partner to work with, you can try splitting the characters between you. Needless to say, two hims or two hers are permissible. The characters are strangers at the start of the story. They should be opposites in some way, like the lovers in the stories by Márquez and Chekhov. But don't make their relationship too implausible; characters who start off by hating each other's guts are a cliché of romantic fiction. Names are not too important at this stage.

Now you have your lovers, where are they going to meet? This question requires a decision about setting, if you haven't thought of one already. Are you going to start with the meeting? Remember short stories cannot waste time slowly building up to the point. If, like Márquez, you delay the meeting, you need to find some other way of getting the reader's attention. His solution is to foreshadow a dramatic ending, building up suspense through anticipation. Is it love at first sight, or something that builds up through the course of the narrative? Be inventive about the first meeting. What would be the least or the most romantic place you could possibly meet? Or ask couples you know how they got together. A friend of mine met his future wife when, slightly tipsy, she slipped and banged her head on the pavement. His first words to her were, 'Are you alright?'

Your next step is to identify the obstacle keeping them apart. As we have discovered, the obstacle could be tangible or psychological. An existing marriage or relationship is one possibility; or social disapproval, cultural differences or geographical distance. It could be a misunderstanding or a lost phone number. Once you have these first pieces of the jigsaw, ask yourself how well they fit together. Does it all make sense? Keep everything as simple as possible. The characters will become more complex once you are actually writing.

Stage 2

When you are ready – immediately or after a few hours or days – make a start. Just write. You do not have to write the story in sequence, starting on Page 1 and ploughing on until the end. If you are stuck on a passage of dialogue or are not sure how to move from one scene to the next, just leave it till later. You will need to decide about viewpoint. The viewpoint can change or it can stay with one person. The narrative could be focalized through one lover or both (see Chapter 4 on 'focalization'). Or the story could be told by another character, perhaps an 'unreliable narrator', for instance someone who is biased against the lovers out of jealousy or some other reason. Are you going to use first- or third-person narration? You could use more than one narrator, showing events through different perspectives. I have implied a linear structure, beginning with the meeting and moving towards some kind of resolution; you could tell it all in flashback.

Another important consideration is your use of tense. Skilfully deployed, the present tense can be punchy and direct, like in Rebecca Brown's story, but it is also easily bogged down in blow-by-blow description. The past tense, used by Chekhov and Márquez, is the traditional tense for storytelling – 'once there was' – but some find writing in the past tense distances their style too much from spoken language. The choices are limitless, and can seem overwhelming. There's no point messing around trying to look clever, but it is worth testing the options, choosing whichever feels most comfortable to write in. Most of these decisions will be reached by trial and error. Later, as you edit, make sure you've been consistent. Don't change tenses randomly or wobble uncertainly between different viewpoints.

Complete a first draft. Your aim is to produce a story of about 2000 words. By its conclusion the couple will have either overcome the obstacle or have been defeated by it. This does not rule out an 'open ending', but the narrative should be tending in one direction or another. Don't use an open ending just because you can't make up your mind.

Beginnings and endings are relatively easy. For some people, the problem is getting stuck in the middle. You've set your characters in motion, and you don't know what to do with them yet. Given the word limit, the action should unfold naturally from the 'obstacle' or build towards it, without involving extraneous plot devices. Take time to develop the relationship between the characters through the kind of descriptive passages we've seen in Chekhov and Márquez. Both writers, in their different ways, layer the narrative with passages conveying mood and atmosphere. Think of your story as something that grows in several dimensions. It is driven forwards, advanced by the plot; but it also thickens – becomes more dense and complex.

Turning points embody the conflicts inherent in the relationship (the letter from Anna's husband), or else they force a crisis (the trip to Anna's home town). If you really do feel the story is going nowhere, introduce something that threatens the status quo or the expectations of at least one of your characters. It doesn't have to be quite as startling as Laura Farina's chastity belt. You might also consider how relationships can shift, and how characters exchange positions during the course of the narrative. What shifts the balance of power in a relationship? In Chapter 6, I showed how Maupassant uses 'plot reversal' in 'Country Living'. Something that was a source of pride becomes a cause of resentment; actions designed to keep the peasant boy with his own family ultimately drive him away. Perhaps the actions of some of your characters also have the opposite effect to the one intended.

How you schedule your time is entirely your decision; I prefer to work in short regular bursts during a first draft. Twenty intensive minutes are more productive than three hours staring at the machine, writing a sentence, deleting it, lying on the floor, and then putting it back in. Don't get too finicky. Nowadays we do not chisel out words on stone tablets; you can always cross it out tomorrow. I have always followed Hemingway's advice, leaving off before I have quite finished what I'm doing. If I scribble down a note reminding me what I was going to write next, I have something to get on with straight away, much more encouraging than returning to a blank page.

Stage 3

After a few days, or preferably a week, read the draft aloud – from the page, not from the screen if, like me, you work on a computer. (I make some suggestions on editing in Activity 8 below.) When you have redrafted again and consider it finished, put the story away for a month or even more, until you can stand back and look at what you've written. Now is the time to ask yourself: what is this story about? Obviously, it is a love story – but what are you saying about love? Try answering that question in a single sentence, as a way to clarifying your ideas. During redrafting, the narrative may have become overcomplicated, or you may have lost sight of your original vision. Changing the story's direction during the writing process is fine, and should be encouraged, but feeling muddled and confused is no good to anyone.

If you are submitting your story to a class or workshop you may not have the luxury of putting your story to one side before one final draft. But I do suggest you let it 'ferment' before submitting it for publication. Stories are never really finished. I carry on wanting to make changes every time I look at my work, even in the middle of a public reading. It is a sign of your growing sophistication as a writer that you set yourself increasingly high standards, constantly dissatisfied with what you've done before. But do make sure you keep a copy of the earliest version. Sometimes you may want to go back to the rawness of the very first draft.

Activity 8   More on editing and revising

Strike out, whenever possible, words qualifying nouns and verbs. You have so many qualifying words that the reader's attention becomes confused and wearied. It's quite clear when I write: 'A man sat down on the grass.' It's clear because it's simple and doesn't hold up one's attention. On the contrary, it's obscure and hard on the brain if I write: 'A tall, narrow-chested, red-bearded man of medium height sat down on the green grass, which had already been trampled underfoot, sat down noiselessly, glancing around timidly and fearfully.' That doesn't sink in immediately, and fiction *has* to sink in immediately, in one second.

(Chekhov 1994: 236–7)

Most editing consists of cutting. As we have seen, Chekhov claimed that he always cut the first and last paragraph. While it can be painful to jettison that lovingly crafted sentence, you will gain more than you lose by trimming excess wordage. Here is a checklist for editing short fiction:

- **Language.** Is the language full of life? Is your own voice coming through, or are you using something second-hand – stiff and over-formal, self-consciously 'literary' or clichéd?
- **Economy.** Do you use twenty words when one would be enough? Do you keep repeating yourself? Are you tautologous ('dark night', 'famous film star')? Do you hold up the narrative with long descriptive passages or background information? Does every sentence go on and on and on until you are bursting for breath when you read it out loud?
- **Objectivity.** The story is an experiment; as its author you are learning something by writing it. So keep an open mind. Don't push a neon-lit message at the reader. Let them reach their own conclusions. Open up political issues rather than laying out a blatant manifesto. In anything other than certain types of horror story, avoid totally monstrous villains. Even Hitler was nice to his dog. Stamp out sensitive poets, saintly housewives married to brutish husbands and anyone remotely goody-goody.
- **Characters.** Do the people come to life? Do we know enough about them – or too much? Are there too many characters for a short story? Does their dialogue sound natural?
- **Viewpoint, tone and voice.** Is the mood of your story sustained? Do you know what effect you want to have on the reader? Are you able to control the tone and the narrative voice, or do they seem uncertain? Is it always clear from whose viewpoint we see the events?
- **Pearls within oysters.** Sometimes there will be one character or incident within your story that rises above the rest. Is this the real story? Should this aspect be developed? You may even decide to lose the rest of the story.
- **Form.** Have you tried to squeeze too much within your story? Did you really want to write a novel?

- **A world of your own.** Is it believable? This is not always a question of whether something would *really* happen. Sometimes even real events or real dialogue fail to ring true in a story. It's more a matter of creating a 'realistic' or fantasy world that is internally consistent and characters whose behaviour is psychologically plausible. Be especially careful with coincidence and with 'twist' endings.
- **Pace and structure.** Do you get straight down to the story or spend ages building up to it? Do you draw the reader in? Are there some passages that need cutting and others developing? Which are the dramatic high points or the turning points in the story? Is the ending too sudden? Does it develop logically or is it just tacked on?

Finally, let me remind you that these points are just guidelines. The best writing is indefinable, and sometimes it breaks all the rules.

Resources

In this section you will find potential outlets for publication, including magazines, competitions and web sites. At the end there are some addresses and web sites you may find handy as sources of information about short-story writing. Use these to keep up to date with new developments and opportunities.

Magazines

This is a selection of magazines open to submissions from unpublished writers. Many literary magazines run regular writers' competitions, and some also publish anthologies and single-author collections. Before sending in your work, read the magazine carefully, checking its submission guidelines and making sure you fit its ethos. Some have a very local identity, others pride themselves on their international status. Some cater for women writers or writers of colour, while others have an experimental or other genre bias. Many US magazines associated with university writing programmes do not accept submissions during the summer months. You can expect to wait several months for a reply. While some welcome e-mail submissions, more and more are refusing to accept them for financial reasons.

Don't forget to double space submissions and proofread carefully. Don't trust your computer to do it all for you. If your spelling isn't great, get someone to help you check through. Enclose a stamped self-addressed envelope or international reply coupons, and a brief letter introducing yourself and your story. Try and make it sound interesting – awaken the editor's curiosity – but remember they will only have time to glance at what you've written. Don't expect magazine editors to provide detailed feedback with a rejection. Again, they simply don't have time to respond personally, although many try to do so. If they are encouraging about your work, send in some more. They don't need to be nice to you; they probably mean what they say.

Literary magazines are born and die every minute, so keep up with these constant changes. Find out the editor's name before submitting your work (this too can change). As well as providing a taste of the magazine, the web sites are an invaluable source of information about writers' groups, small presses, events and the craft of writing. Subscribe; when you read these magazines and visit their web sites you are joining the writing community. Agents and publishers look for exciting new talent in the magazines.

UK and Ireland print magazines

Includes titles with online editions. Virtual magazines and e-zines are listed separately.

Ambit, 17 Priory Gardens, London N6 5QY, www.ambit magazine.co.uk

Brittle Star, 41 Whitton, 89 King Henry's Road, London NW3 3RE, www.brittlestar.org.uk

Cambrensis, 41 Heol Fach, Cornelly, Bridgend, Wales CF33 4LN, www.geocities.com/storywales

Chapman, 4 Broughton Place, Edinburgh EH1 3RX, www.chapman-pub.co.uk

Chroma, www.gaymenwriting.co.uk

Critical Quarterly, School of English, Queen's Building, The Queen's Drive, Exeter EX4 4QY, www.criticalquarterly.com. (US address: Department of English, University of Pittsburgh, Pittsburgh PA 15260.)

The Eildon Tree, Library Headquarters, St Mary's Mill, Selkirk TD7 5EW, www.eildontree.org.uk

The Erotic Review, 30 Cleveland Street, London W1T 4JD, www.theeroticreview.co.uk

Interzone, www.ttapress.com/IZhtml

The Ladder Review, theladderreview@yahoo.co.uk

London Magazine, 32 Addison Grove, London W4 1ER.

Mslexia, P.O. Box 656, Newcastle upon Tyne, NE99 1PZ,
www.mslexia.co.uk

The New Writer, P.O. Box 60, Cranbrook, Kent TN17 27R,
www.thenewwriter.com

Northwords, P.O. Box 5725, Dingwall, Ross-shire IV15 9WJ,
www.northwords.co.uk

Pretext, Pen & Inc. Press, School of English and American Studies,
University of East Anglia, Norwich, Norfolk NR4 7TJ,
www.inpressbooks.co.uk/penandic

Prospect, Prospect Publishing, 2 Bloomsbury Place, London WC1A
2QA, www.prospect-magazine.co.uk

QWF, P.O. Box 1768, Rugby CV21 42A.

Riot Angel, 63 Colomb Street, Greenwich, London SE10 9E2,
www.riotangel.co.uk

Scheherezade, 14 Queens Park Rise, Brighton BN2 9ZF,
www.schez.co.uk

Southword, The Munster Literature Centre, Frank O'Connor House,
84 Douglas Street, Cork, Ireland, www.munsterlit.ie

Spoiled Ink, www.spoiledink.com

Stand, School of English, Leeds University, Leeds LS2 9JT,
www.people.vcu.edn~dlatane/stand.html

The Third Alternative, 5 St Martins Lane, Witcham, Ely CB6 2LB,
www.ttapress.com

Wasafiri, Department of English and Drama, Queen Mary, University of
London, Mile End Road, London E1 4NS, www.wasafiri.org

Zembla, 61A Ledbury Road, London W11 2AL,
www.zemblamagazine.com

US and Canada print magazines

Alaska Quarterly Review, University of Alaska Anchorage, 3211
Providence Drive, Anchorage, AK 99508, www.uaa.alaska.edu/aqr

Amazing Stories, www.paizo.com/amazing.shtml

Analog, 475 Park Avenue South, New York, NY 10016,
www.analogsf.com

Antioch Review, P.O. Box 148, Yellow Springs, OH 45387,
www.review.antioch.edu

Ascent, English Department, Concordia College, 901 8th Street South, Moorhead, MN 56562, www.cord.edu/dept/english/ascent

The Atlantic Monthly, 77 North Washington Street, Boston, MA 02114, www.theatlantic.com

Bellevue Literary Review, Department of Medicine, Room OBV-61, NYU School of Medicine, 550 First Avenue, New York, NY 10016, www.blreview.org

Boulevard Magazine, 6614 Clayton Road, P.O. Box 325, Richmond Heights, MO 63117, www.richardburgin.com

Callaloo, English Department, 322 Bryan Hall, University of Virginia, Charlottesville, VA 22904-4121, www.xroads.virginia.edu/~public/callaloo/home/callaloohome.htm

Carolina Quarterly, Greenlaw Hall CB#3520, University of North Carolina, Chapel Hill, NC 27599–3520, www.unc.edu/depts/cqonline

Chattahoochee Review, 2101 Womack Road, Dunwoody, GA. 30338–4497, www.chattahoochee-review.org/index.htm

Colorado Review, Department of English, Colorado State University, Fort Collins, CO 80523, www.coloradoreview.com

Conjunctions, 21 East 10th Street, New York, NY 10003, www.conjunctions.com

Contrary, P.O. Box 4044, Merchandise Mart, Chicago, IL 60654–4044, www.contrarymagazine.com

Crab Orchard Review, Southern Illinois University at Carbondale, Carbondale, IL 62901–4503, www.siu.edu/~crborchd

Cut Bank, English Department, University of Montana, Missoula, MT 59812, www.umt.edu/cutbank

Epicenter, P.O. Box 367, Riverside, CA 92502, www.epicentermagazine.org

Epoch, 251 Goldwin Smith Hall, Cornell University, Ithaca, NY 14853–3201, www.arts.cornell.edu/english/epoch.html

Faultline, English and Comparative Literature Department, University of California-Irvine, Irvine, CA 92697–2650, www.humanities.uci.edu/faultline

Fence, 14 Fifth Avenue, 1A, New York, NY 1001 1, www.fencemag.com

Florida Review, English Department, University of Central Florida, Orlando, FL 32816, www.flreview.com

Fourteen Hills, Creative Writing Department, San Francisco State University, 1600 Holloway Avenue, San Francisco, CA 94132–1722, www.mercury.sfsu.edu/~hills/welcome.html

Georgia Review, University of Georgia, Athens, GA 30602–9009,
www.uga.edu/garev

Gettysburg Review, Gettysburg College, Gettysburg, PA 17325,
www.gettysburg.edu/academics/gettysburg_review

Glimmer Train Stories, 710 SW Madison Street, Suite 504, Portland, OR
97205–2900, www.glimmertrain.com

The Idaho Review, Boise State University, English Department, 1910
University Drive, Boise, ID 83725,
www.english.boisestate.edu/idahoreview

Image, 3307 Third Avenue West, Seattle, WA 98119,
www.imagejournal.org

Indiana Review, 465 Ballantine Hall, 1020 E. Kirkwood Avenue,
Bloomington, IN 47405–7103, www.indiana.edu/~inreview/index.html

Iowa Review, 308 English/Philosophy Building, University of Iowa, Iowa
City, IA 52242–1492, www.uiowa.edu/~iareview

Kalliope, Florida Community College at Jacksonville, 3939 Roosevelt
Boulevard, Jacksonville, FL 32205,
www.fccj.org/kalliope/kalliope.htm

Kenyon Review, Kenyon College, Gambier, OH 43022,
www.kenyonreview.org

Literal Latté, Suite 240, 61 East 8th Street, New York, NY 10003,
www.literal-latte.com

Literary Review, Farleigh Dickinson University, 285 Madison Avenue,
Madison, NJ 07940, www.theliteraryreview.org

McSweeney's Quarterly, 826 Valencia Street, San Fransisco, CA 94110,
www.mcsweeneys.net

Malahat Review, University of Victoria, P.O. Box 1700, Victoria, British
Columbia V8W 2Y2, Canada, www.web.uvic.ca/malahat

Manoa, English Department, University of Hawaii, Honolulu, HI 96822,
www.hawaii.edu/mjournal

Massachusetts Review, South College, University of Massachusetts, P.O.
Box 37140, Amherst, MA 01003–7140, www.massreview.org

Minnesota Review, English Department, University of
Missouri-Columbia, 110 Tate Hall, Columbia, MO 65211,
www.theminnesotareview.org

Missouri Review, 1507 Hillcrest Hall, University of Missouri, Columbia,
MO 65211, www.missourireview.org

Natural Bridge, English Department, University of Missouri-St. Louis,
8001 Natural Bridge Road, St Louis, MO 63121, www.umsl.edu/~natural

New Delta Review, English Department, Louisiana State University, Baton Rouge, LA 70803–5001, www.english.lsu.edu/journals/ndr

New England Review, Middlebury College, Middlebury, VT 05753, www.middlebury.edu/~nereview

New Letters, University of Missouri-Kansas City, 5100 Rockhill Road, Kansas City, MO 64110, www.newletters.org

New Orleans Review, P.O. Box 195, Loyola University, New Orleans, LA 70118, www.loyno.edu/~noreview

The New Yorker, 4 Times Square, New York, NY 10036, www.newyorker.com

NFG, Shepphard Centre, P.O. Box 43112, Toronto, Ontario, M2N 6N1, Canada, www.nfg.ca

Nimrod, University of Tulsa, 600 South College, Tulsa, OK 74104–3189, www.utulsa.edu/nimrod

North American Review, University of Northern Iowa, 1222 West 27th Street, Cedar Falls, IA 50614–0156, www.webdelsol.com/northamreview/nar

Notre Dame Review, Creative Writing Program, English Department, University of Notre Dame, Notre Dame, IN 46556, www.nd.edu/~ndr/review.htm

One Story, P.O. Box 1326, New York, NY 10156, www.one-story.com

Ontario Review, 9 Honey Brook Drive, Princeton, NJ 08540, www.ontarioreviewpress.com

Open City Magazine, 270 Lafayette Street, Suite 1412, New York, NY 10012–3327, www.opencity.org

Orchid, 3096 Williamsburg, Ann Arbor, MI 48108–2026, www.orchidlit.org

Oyster Boy Review, P.O. Box 77842, San Francisco, CA 94107–0842, www.oysterboyreview.com

Paris Review, 541 East 72nd Street, New York, NY 10021, www.parisreview.com

Ploughshares, Emerson College, 120 Boylston Street, Boston, MA 02116–4624, www.pshares.org

Prairie Fire, 423–100 Arthur Street, Winnipeg, Manitoba, R3B 1H3, Canada, www.prairiefire.mb.ca

Prairie Schooner, 201 Andrews Hall, University of Nebraska, Lincoln, NE 68588–0334, www.unl.edu/schooner/psmain.htm

Quarterly West, 317 Olpin Union Hall, University of Utah, Salt Lake City, UT 84112, webdelsol.com/quarterly_west

River City, English Department, University of Memphis, Memphis,
TN 38152–6176, www.people.memphis.edu/~rivercity

Sewanee Review, University of the South, 735 University Avenue,
Sewanee, TN 37383–1000, www.sewanee.edu/sreview/home.html

The Sink, www.thesinkmag.com

Southeast Review, English Department, Florida State University,
Tallahassee, FL 32311,
www.english.fsu.edu/southeastreview/default.htm

Southwest Review, Southern Methodist University, 307 Fondren Library
West, Dallas, TX 75275, www.southwestreview.org

The Strand Magazine, P.O. Box 1418, Birmingham, MI 48012–1418,
www.strandmagazine.com

The Sun, 107 North Roberson Street, Chapel Hill, NC 27516,
www.thesunmagazine.org

Swink, 244 Fifth Avenue #2722, New York, NY 10001,
www.swinkmag.com

Third Coast, English Department, Western Michigan University,
Kalamazoo, MI 49008–5092, www.wmich.edu/thirdcoast

The Threepenny Review, P.O. Box 9131, Berkeley, CA 94709,
www.threepennyreview.com

Tin House, P.O. Box 10500, Portland, OR 97296–0500,
www.tinhouse.com

Transition Magazine, W. E. B. DuBois Institute, Harvard University,
69 Dunster Street, Cambridge, MA 02138,
www.transitionmagazine.com

Virginia Quarterly Review, 1 West Range, P.O. Box 400223,
Charlottesville, VA 22903–4223, www.vqronline.org

Washington Square, Creative Writing Program, New York University,
19 University Place, 2nd Floor, New York, NY 10003–4556,
www.nyu.edu/fas/program/cwp/wsr

Weird Tales, P.O. Box 2988, Radford, VA 24143–2988,
www.weird-tales.com

Western Humanities Review, University of Utah, English Department,
255 South Central Campus Drive, Room 3500, Salt Lake City, UT
84112–0494, www.hum.utah.edu/whr

Zoetrope: All-Story, 916 Kearny Street, San Francisco, CA 94133,
www.all-story.com

Online magazines

Absinthe Literary Review, www.absinthe-literary-review.com
Asimov's Magazine, www.asimovs.com
Babel, www.towerofbabel.com
The Barcelona Review, www.barcelonareview.com
Boomerang, www.boomerang.co.uk
Carve, www.carvezine.com
East of the Web, www.short-stories.co.uk
Eclectica, www.eclectica.org
Failbetter, www.failbetter.com
Gothic.Net, www.gothic.net
Infinity Plus, www.infinityplus.co.uk
Nerve, www.nerve.com
NU Leaves, www.nuleaves.com
Open Wide, www.openwidemagazine.co.uk
The Pedestal Magazine, www.the pedestalmagazine.com
La Petite Zine, www.lapetitezine.org
Pulp, www.pulp.net
The Richmond Review, www.richmondreview.co.uk
Stride, www.stridemagazine.co.uk
Tarpaulin Sky, www.tarpaulinsky.com
3 a.m., www.3ammagazine.com
West 47, www.galwayartscentre.i.e/west47/index.html
Word Riot, www.wordriot.org
Xaxx, www.xaxx.net
Xconnect: Writers of the Information Age,
   www.ccat.sas.upenn.edu/xconnect

Prizes

Nearly all of the US magazines run competitions for unpublished stories, many of them very prestigious. *The Atlantic Monthly* also runs an online student-writing contest. Check the web sites for details. In Britain, *Stand* magazine runs a well-established competition. Other major UK and Ireland prizes are listed below.

The Asham Award, The Adminstrator, Asham Trust, Town Hall,
   High Street, Lewes BN17 2QS,
      www.wordup.co.uk/awardsandprizes/old/asham.htm (Women only.)

The Bridport Prize, Bridport Arts Centre, South Street, Dorset DT6 3NR, www.bridportprize.org

Fish Short Story Competition, Durrus, Co. Cork, Ireland, www.fishpublishing.com

International PEN David T. K. Wong Prize for Short Fiction, www.englishpen.org/prizes/davidtkwongprize

Sean O'Faolain Short Story Competition, The Munster Literature Centre, Frank O'Connor House, 84 Douglas Street, Cork, Ireland, www.munsterlit.ie

V. S. Pritchett Memorial Prize, The Royal Society of Literature, Somerset House, Strand, London WC2R 1LA.

Useful organizations and databases

BBC Get Writing web site. Run by the British Broadcasting Corporation, provides advice, information on competitions and openings for new talent in short fiction as well as scriptwriting. www.bbc.co.uk/dna/getwriting

Black Lace Books erotica-readers.com/ERA/G/Blacklace.htm

The Branching Out web site lists small British-based independent publishers, www.branching-out.net/independent

Council of Literary Magazines and Presses is a US-based forum, with useful listings for writers, www.clmp.org

The Electronic Literature Organization facilitates and promotes writing, reading and publishing in electronic form, www.eliterature.org

The Federation of Worker Writers and Community Publishers, P.O. Box 540, Burslem, Stoke-on-Trent ST6 DR. Contact fwcp@mcmail.com for local groups.

Save Our Short Story campaign backed by the British Arts Council to promote the short-story form. www.saveourshortstory.org.uk

The Frank O'Connor International Festival of the Short Story. The Munster Literature Centre, Frank O'Connor House, 84 Douglas Street, Cork, Ireland, www.munsterlit.ie

Litline. Illinois-based web site for the literary community, with many national and international links, www.litline.org

The Open College of the Arts. Distance-learning courses, including specialized short-story course, with one-to-one feedback from published writers, www.oca-uk.com

Web del Sol, www.webdelsol.com

Word Up, www.wordup.co.uk

Writing World, www.writing-world.com

Bibliography

Achebe, Chinua (1982) *Girls at War and Other Stories*, London: Heinemann.

Aldiss, Brian (2001) *Supertoys Last All Summer Long and Other Stories of Future Time*, London: Orbit.

Andersen, Hans Christian (1992) *Fairy Tales*, London: Everyman.

Aronofsky, Darren (1999) *Pi*, London: Faber & Faber.

Asimov, Isaac (1984) *The Complete Robot*, London: Panther.

Asimov, Isaac (1990) *The Complete Stories VI*, New York: Doubleday.

Atkinson, Kate (2003a) *Not the End of the World*, London: Doubleday.

Atkinson, Kate (2003b) 'Putting the fun back into fiction', *Guardian*, Saturday Review, 21 June.

Atwood, Margaret (1996) *Bluebeard's Egg*, London: Vintage.

Atwood, Margaret (2002) *Negotiating with the Dead: A Writer on Writing*, Cambridge: Cambridge University Press.

Ballard, J. G. (2002) *The Complete Short Stories*, London: Flamingo.

Barnes, Julian (1990) *A History of the World in 10½ Chapters*, London: Picador.

Bigsby, Christopher (2000) *Writers in Conversation: Volume One*, Norwich: EAS.

Blackburn, Michael, Jon Silkin and Lorna Tracy (1984) *Stand One: Winners of the Stand Magazine Short Story Competition*, London: Gollancz.

Blincoe, Nicholas and Matt Thorne (eds) (2001) *All Hail the New Puritans*, London: Fourth Estate.

Boccaccio, Giovanni (1972) *The Decameron*, trans. G. H. McWilliam, Harmondsworth: Penguin.

Borges, Jorge Luis (1971) *Labyrinths*, Harmondsworth: Penguin.

Bowen, Elizabeth (1999) *Collected Stories*, London: Vintage.

Boylan, Clare (1993) *The Agony and the Ego: The Art and Strategy of Fiction Writing Explored*, Harmondsworth: Penguin.

Bradbury, Ray (1980) *The Stories of Ray Bradbury*, New York: Knopf.

Bradfield, Scott (1993) *Greetings from Earth: New and Collected Stories*, London: Picador.

Brite, Poppy Z. (ed.) (1997) *Love in Vein II*, New York: HarperCollins.

Broks, Paul (2003) *Into the Silent Land*, London: Atlantic.

Brown, Molly (2001) *Bad Timing and Other Stories*, Abingdon: Big Engine.

Brown, Rebecca (1989) 'Dr Frankenstein, I Presume' in *Storia 2: Love*, London: Pandora, pp. 1–7.

Butler, Robert Olen (1997) *Tabloid Dreams*, London: Minerva.

Byatt, A. S. (2003) *The Little Black Book of Stories*, London: Chatto & Windus.

Calvino, Italo (1985) *Marcovaldo*, trans. William Weaver, London: Vintage.

Calvino, Italo (1993) *Under the Jaguar Sun*, trans. William Weaver, London: Vintage.

Calvino, Italo (1996) *Six Memos for the Next Millennium*, trans. Patrick Creagh, London: Vintage.

Calvino, Italo (1997) *The Literature Machine*, trans. Patrick Creagh, London: Vintage.

Campbell, Ramsey (2003) *Scared Stiff: Tales of Sex and Death*, New York: Tor.

Carter, Angela (1981) *The Bloody Chamber and Other Stories*, Harmondsworth: Penguin.

Carter, Angela (ed.) (1986) *Wayward Girls and Wicked Women*, London: Virago.

Carver, Raymond (1994) *Fires*, London: Harvill.

Carver, Raymond (1998) *Where I'm Calling From: The Selected Stories*, London: Harvill.

Cassini, Marco and Martina Testa (eds) (2003) *The Burned Children of America*, London: Hamish Hamilton.

Chabon, Michael (ed.) (2003) *McSweeney's Mammoth Treasury of Thrilling Tales*, New York: Vintage.

Chaucer, Geoffrey (1996) *The Canterbury Tales*, Harmondsworth: Penguin.

Chekhov, Anton (1971) *Lady with Lapdog and Other Stories*, trans. David Magarshack, Harmondsworth: Penguin.

Chekhov, Anton (1986) *The Fiancée and Other Stories*, trans. Ronald Wilks, Harmondsworth: Penguin.

Chekhov, Anton (1994) *A Life In Letters*, trans. and ed. Gordon McVay, London: The Folio Society.

Chiang, Ted (2002) *Stories of Your Life and Others*, New York: Orb.

Clarkson, Ann (2003) 'Morning Chemistry', *Mslexia 18*, pp. 33–4.

Coen, Ethan (1999) *Gates of Eden*, London: Anchor.

Conan Doyle, Arthur (1990) *When the World Screamed and Other Stories*, San Francisco, CA: Chronicle Books.

Conan Doyle, Arthur (1994) *The Adventures of Sherlock Holmes*, Harmondsworth: Penguin.

Conrad, Joseph (1998) *Heart of Darkness and Other Tales*, ed. Cedric Watts, Oxford: Oxford University Press.

Cox, Ailsa (1996) 'Writing the Self' in John Singleton and Mary Luckhurst (eds) The *Creative Writing Handbook*, London: Macmillan.

Dahl, Roald (1991) *The Collected Stories of Roald Dahl*, Harmondsworth: Penguin.

Damasio, Antonio (2000) *The Feeling of What Happens: Body, Emotion and the Making of Consciousness*, London: Vintage.

Dawood, N. J. (trans.) (1974) *Tales from the Thousand and One Nights*, Harmondsworth: Penguin.

Desai, Anita (2001) *Diamond Dust*, London: Vintage.

Dick, Philip K. (1995) *The Shifting Realities of Philip K. Dick*, ed. Lawrence Sutin, New York: Vintage.

Dick, Philip K. (2003) *We Can Remember It For You Wholesale*, London: Gollancz.

Dinesen, Isak (1993) *Seven Gothic Tales*, Harmondsworth: Penguin.

Edwards, Martin (1997) 'Successful Crime Writing', *Writing Magazine*, February–March: 53.

Edwards, Martin (ed.) (2003) *Mysterious Pleasures*, London: Little, Brown.

Fitzgerald, F. Scott (1974) *Collected Stories*, Harmondsworth: Penguin.

Forster, E. M. (1963) *Aspects of the Novel*, Harmondsworth: Penguin.

Freud, Sigmund (1990) 'Creative Writers and Day-Dreaming', in Albert Dickson (ed.) *Art and Literature*, trans. James Strachey, Harmondsworth: Penguin, pp.129–41.

Freudenberger, Nell (2003) *Lucky Girls*, London: Picador.

Funder, Anna (2004) *Stasiland: Stories From Behind the Berlin Wall*, London: Granta.

Gallant, Mavis (2004) *The Selected Stories of Mavis Gallant*, London: Bloomsbury.

Galloway, Jane (1996) *Where You Find It*, London: Jonathan Cape.

Gapper, Frances (2003) 'Interview: Ali Smith', *Mslexia 18*: 14–16.

Gibson, William (1995) *Burning Chrome*, London: HarperCollins.

Gilbert, Sandra M. and Susan Gubar (1985) *The Norton Anthology of Literature by Women*, New York: W. W. Norton.

Givner, Joan (1983) *The Life of Katherine Anne Porter*, London: Jonathan Cape.

Goldberg, Natalie (1986) *Writing Down the Bones*, Boston, MA and London: Shambhala.

Gordimer, Nadine (1991) '1991 Nobel Lecture', available online: www.nobel.se/literature/laureates/1991/gordimer-lecture.html (accessed 25 July 2004).

Green, Jen and Sarah Lefanu (eds) (1985) *Despatches from the Frontiers of the Female Mind*, London: The Women's Press.

Greene, Graham (1980) *Ways of Escape*, London: The Bodley Head.

Greene, Graham (1999) *A Sort of Life*, London: Vintage.

Haffenden, John (1986) *Novelists in Interview*, London: Methuen.

Hammett, Dashiell (2002) *Nightmare Town: Twenty Long Unavailable Stories*, London: Picador.

Highsmith, Patricia (2002) *Little Tales of Misogyny*, New York: W. W. Norton.

Homer (1997) *The Odyssey*, trans. Robert Fagles, Harmondsworth: Penguin.

Irving, Washington (2000) *The Legend of Sleepy Hollow*, Harmondsworth: Penguin.

Isaacs, Neil D. (1990) *Grace Paley: A Study of the Short Fiction*, Boston, MA: Trayne.

James, Edward (1994) *Science Fiction in the Twentieth Century:* Oxford: Oxford University Press.

James, Henry (1998) *The Turn of the Screw*, Oxford: Oxford University Press.

James, Henry (2001) *Ghost Stories*, Ware: Wordsworth.

James, M. R.(1993) *Collected Ghost Stories*, Ware: Wordsworth.

Jones, Stephen (ed.) (2002) *The Mammoth Book of Best New Horror*, London: Constable & Robinson.

Joyce, James (1961) *Dubliners*, Harmondsworth: Penguin.

Joyce, James (1977) *Ulysses*, Harmondsworth: Penguin.

Joyce, Michael (2003) (available online): 'Twelve Blue. Story in Eight Bars', www.eastgate.com/twelveblue/welcome.html (accessed 21 August 2003).

Kafka, Franz (1992) *The Transformation and Other Stories*, trans. Malcolm Pasley, Harmondsworth: Penguin.

Karnezis, Panos (2003) *Little Infamies*, London: Vintage.

Keillor, Garrison (1988) *Lake Wobegon Days*, London: Faber & Faber.

Kelman, James (1995) *Not Not While the Giro and Other Stories*, London: Minerva.

Kincaid, Jamaica (1997) *Annie John*, London: Vintage.

King, Stephen (2001) *On Writing*, London: Hodder & Stoughton.

King, Stephen (2002) *Everything's Eventual*, London: Hodder & Stoughton.

Klíma, Ivan (1989) *My First Loves*, trans. Ewald Osers, Harmondsworth: Penguin.

Lahiri, Jhumpa (2000) *Interpreter of Maladies*, London: Flamingo.

Lamb, Charles and Mary Lamb (1995) *Tales from Shakespeare*, Harmondsworth: Penguin.

Le Guin, Ursula (1990) *Buffalo Gals and Other Animal Presences*, London: Gollancz.

Lem, Stanislaw (1991) *Imaginary Magnitude*, trans. Marc E. Heine, London: Mandarin.

Levy, Andrew (1993) *The Culture and Commerce of the American Short Story*, Cambridge, MA: Cambridge University Press.

London, Jack (1990) *The Call of the Wild, White Fang and Other Stories*, Oxford: Oxford University Press.

Lovecraft, H. P. (1998) 'Supernatural Horror in Literature' in Clive Bloom (ed.) *Gothic Horror: A Reader's Guide from Poe to King and Beyond*, Basingstoke: Macmillan.

Lovecraft, H. P. (1999) *The Call of Cthulhu and Other Weird Stories*, Harmondsworth: Penguin.

McCabe, Patrick (1999) *Mondo Desperado*, London: Picador.

McCaffery, Larry (1990) *Across the Wounded Galaxies: Interviews with Contemporary American Science Fiction Writers*, Urbana, IL: University of Illinois Press.

MacLeod, Alistair (2002) *Island: Collected Stories*, London: Vintage.

Manguel, Alberto (1996) *A History of Reading*, London: Flamingo.

Mann, Thomas (1997) *Death in Venice*, trans. David Luke, London: Minerva.

Mansfield, Katherine (1984) *The Collected Short Stories*, Harmondsworth: Penguin.

Mansfield, Katherine (1989) *Selected Letters*, Oxford: Clarendon Press.

Márquez, Gabriel García (1991) *Collected Stories*, trans. Gregory Rabassa and J. S. Bernstein, London: Jonathan Cape.

Maupassant, Guy de (1990) *A Day in the Country and Other Stories*, trans. David Coward, Oxford: Oxford University Press.

Maupassant, Guy de (2001) 'The Novel', introduction to *Pierre et Jean*, trans. Julie Mead, Oxford: Oxford University Press: 3–14.

Miller, Judith (ed.) (1984) *The Art of Alice Munro: Saying the Unsayable*, Ontario: University of Waterloo Press.

Mitchell, David (1999) *Ghostwritten*, London: Sceptre.

Mitchell, Pradima (2003) *Anansi and Brer Rabbit Stories*, Harlow: Pearson Schools Longman.

Mühling, Jens (2003) 'The Permanent Exile of W. G. Sebald', *Pretext* 7: 15–26.

Munro, Alice (1984) *Lives of Girls and Women*, Harmondsworth: Penguin.

Munro, Alice (1987) *Something I've Been Meaning to Tell You*, Harmondsworth: Penguin.

Munro, Alice (1988) *The Beggar Maid*, Harmondsworth: Penguin.

Munro, Alice (1995) *Open Secrets*, London: Vintage.

Munro, Alice (1998) *The Love of a Good Woman*, London: Vintage.

Munro, Alice (2001) *Hateship, Friendship, Loveship, Courtship, Marriage*, London: Chatto & Windus.

Nabokov, Vladimir (1980) *Lectures on Literature*, ed. Fredson Bowers, London: Weidenfeld & Nicolson.

Narayan, R. K. (1987) *Under the Banyan Tree*, Harmondsworth: Penguin.

Narayan, R. K. (1995) *Malgudi Days*, Harmondsworth: Penguin.

Ngũgĩ Wa Thiong'o (1983) *Secret Lives*, London: Heinemann.

Nin, Anaïs (2000) *Delta of Venus*, Harmondsworth: Penguin.

O'Brien, Tim (1991) *The Things They Carried*, London: Flamingo.

O'Connor, Frank (1963) *The Lonely Voice: A Study of the Short Story*, Cleveland, OH: The World Publishing Company.

O'Mahony, John (2003) 'King of Bog Gothic', interview with Patrick

McCabe, *Guardian*, Saturday Review, 30 August, available online: guardian.co.uk/books (accessed 25 July 2004).

Oates, Joyce Carol (1998) 'The Origins and Art of the Short Story' in Barbara Lounsberry, Susan Lohafer, Mary Rohrberger, Stephen Pett and R. C. Feddersen (eds) *The Tales We Tell: Perspectives on the Short Story*, Westport, CT: Greenwood Press.

Oates, Joyce Carol (2002) *Where Are You Going, Where Have You Been? Stories of Young America*, Princeton, NJ: Ontario Review Press.

Opie, Iona and Peter (1967) *The Lore and Language of Schoolchildren*, London: Oxford University Press.

Opie, Iona and Peter (1974) *The Classic Fairy Tales*, Oxford: Oxford University Press.

Orwell, George (2003) *Shooting an Elephant and Other Stories*, Harmondsworth: Penguin.

Paley, Grace (1980) *The Little Disturbances of Man*, London: Virago.

Park, Christine and Caroline Heaton (eds) (1992) *Caught in a Story: Contemporary Fairytales and Fables*, London: Vintage.

Poe, Edgar Allan (1966) in *Tales, Poems and Essays*, London: Collins.

Poe, Edgar Allan (1994) *Selected Tales*, Harmondsworth: Penguin.

Porter, Katherine Anne (1985) *The Collected Stories*, London: Virago.

Poynting, Jeremy (2003) 'The Caribbean Short Story', available online: www.peepaltreepress.com/features.asp (accessed 25 July 2004).

Prior, Amy (ed.) (2003) *Strictly Casual: Fiction by Women on Love*, London: Serpent's Tail.

Proulx, Annie (1999) *Close Range: Wyoming Stories*, London: Fourth Estate.

Reaves, Michael and John Pelan (eds) (2003) *Shadows over Baker Street*, New York: Ballantine.

Rendell, Ruth (1994) *Collected Short Stories*, London: Arrow.

Royle, Nicholas (ed.) (1996) *The Tiger Garden: A Book of Writers' Dreams*, London: Serpent's Tail.

Salkey, Andrew (ed.) (1998) *Carribean Folk Tales and Legends*, London: Bogle-L'Ouverture.

Sanger, J. (ed.) (2004) *Sexy Shorts for Summer*, Pembroke: Accent Press.

Schnitzler, Arthur (1999) *Dream Story*, trans. J. M. Q. Davies, Harmondsworth: Penguin.

Sebald, W. G. (2002) *The Emigrants*, trans. Michael Hulse, London: Vintage.

Shippey, Tom (2003) *The Oxford Book of Science Fiction Stories*, Oxford: Oxford University Press.

Simpson, Helen (2001) *Hey Yeah Right Get a Life*, London: Vintage.

Smith, Ali (2003) 'May' in *The Whole Story and Other Stories*, London: Hamish Hamilton.

Stevenson, Robert Louis (1920) *Essays in the Art of Writing*, London: Chatto & Windus.

Stevenson, Robert Louis (1950) *RLS: An Omnibus*, ed. G. B. Stern, London: Cassell.

Stevenson, Robert Louis (1994) *Dr. Jekyll and Mr. Hyde*, Harmondsworth: Penguin.

Swift, Jonathan (1996) *A Modest Proposal*, New York: Dover.

Tan, Amy (1991) *The Joy Luck Club*, London: Vintage.

Trevor, William (1996) *After Rain*, London: Viking.

Twain, Mark (2000) *Cannibalism in the Cars: The Best of Twain's Humorous Sketches*, London: Prion.

Updike, John (2004) *The Early Stories 1953–1975*, London: Hamish Hamilton.

Walker, Alice (1987) *You Can't Keep a Good Woman Down*, London: The Women's Press.

Wells, H. G. (2000) *The Complete Short Stories of H. G. Wells*, London: Phoenix Press.

Welsh, Irvine (1999) *Trainspotting*, London: Vintage.

Wharton, Edith (1997) *The Ghost Stories of Edith Wharton*, New York: Scribner.

Wodehouse, P. G. (2003) *Weekend Wodehouse*, London: Pimlico.

Woolf, Virginia (1976) *Moments of Being: Unpublished Autobiographical Writings*, London: Chatto & Windus for Sussex University Press.

Yorke, Margaret (1994) *Pieces of Justice*, London: Warner-Futura.

Index

Related titles from Routledge

Creative Writing and the New Humanities
Paul Dawson

'It is rare to have a text that not only meets a very real need academically, but one that is written with heartening persuasion and clarity. This is clearly excellent scholarship.'
David Morley, *Director – University of Warwick Writing Programme*

Discussions about Creative Writing have tended to revolve around the perennial questions 'can writing be taught?' and 'should it be taught?'

In this ambitious new book, Paul Dawson carries the debate far beyond the usual arguments and demonstrates that the discipline of Creative Writing developed as a series of pedagogic responses to the long-standing 'crisis' in literary studies. He traces the emergence of Creative Writing alongside the New Criticism in American universities; examines the writing workshop in relation to theories of creativity and literary criticism; and analyses the evolution of Creative Writing pedagogy alongside and in response to the rise of 'theory' in America, England and Australia.

Paul Dawson's thoroughly researched and engaging book provides a fresh perspective on the importance of Creative Writing to the 'new humanities' and makes a major contribution to current debates about the role of the writer as public intellectual.

Hb: 0–415–33220–6
Pb: 0–415–33221–4

Available at all good bookshops
For ordering and further information please visit
www.routledgeclassics.com

Related titles from Routledge

Creative Writing: A Workbook with Readings
Edited by Linda Anderson
Co-published with the Open University

'A course book as good as this is a rare event'
David Morley, Director of Warwick Writing Programme

'With so many angles covered and contributors' insights included, this workbook avoids imparting systematised guidelines for writing creatively. A valuable source for dipping in and out of.'
Russell Celyn Jones, novelist, critic and staff reviewer for the Times, based at Birkbeck, University of London.

Creative Writing: A Workbook with Readings is a complete writing course that will jump-start your writing and guide you through your first steps towards publication.

Suitable for use by students, tutors, writers' groups or writers working alone, this book offers:
- a practical and inspiring section on the creative process, showing you how to stimulate your creativity and use your memory and experience in inventive ways;
- in-depth coverage of the most popular forms of writing: fiction, poetry and life writing, including biography and autobiography, giving you practice in all three forms so that you discover and develop your strengths;
- a sensible, up-to-date guide to going public, to help you edit your work to a professional standard and identify and approach suitable publishers;
- a distinctive collection of exciting exercises, spread throughout the workbook to spark your imagination and increase your technical flexibility and control;
- a substantial array of illuminating readings, bringing together extracts from contemporary and classical writings to demonstrate a range of techniques that you can use or adapt in your own work.

Creative Writing: A Workbook with Readings presents a unique opportunity to benefit from the advice and experience of a team of published authors who have also taught successful writing courses at a wide range of institutions, helping large numbers of new writers to develop their talents and their abilities to evaluate and polish their work to professional standards.

Hb: 0–415–37242–9
Pb: 0–415–37243–7

Available at all good bookshops
For ordering and further information please visit
www.routledgeclassics.com

Related titles from Routledge

Playwriting: A practical Guide
Noël Greig

'I have spent half my career waiting for this book to be written. Noël Greig is the original great communicator, playwright, mentor, tutor, support, coach and inspiration. His knowledge and ability should be listed as a national asset. Noël's mantra is "only connect" and I have yet to find an individual who has met him, and has failed to do this on a thousand and one levels. **Buy this book and prepare to be wowed.**'
Ola Animashawun, *Associate Director, Young Writers Programme, The Royal Court Theatre, London.*

What makes a story work?

Playwriting offers a practical guide to the creation of text for live performance, and contains a wealth of exercises for all individuals and groups involved in making theatre. It can be used in a range of contexts: either as a step-by-step guide to the creation of an individual play, as a handy resource for a teacher or workshop leader, or as a stimulus for the group-devised play. The result of Noël Greig's thirty years' experience as a playwright, actor, director and teacher, *Playwriting i*s the ideal handbook for anyone who engages with playwriting and is ultimately concerned with creating a story and bringing it to life on the stage.

Hb: 0–415–31043–1
Pb: 0–415–31044–X

Available at all good bookshops
For ordering and further information please visit
www.routledgeclassics.com